Augus

To Mary Ellen —

A Devotee of Great
Literature, of Fine Arts, and
of our cherished 30 year
friendship.

May The Lyrics Of Your Life
Accompany
A Beautiful Melody

Love,

Barbara - Jo

PLAY ME A SONG

Barbara-Jo
Lucchine Kruczek

iUniverse, Inc.
New York   Bloomington

Play Me A Song

iUniverse books may be ordered through booksellers or by contacting:

iUniverse
1663 Liberty Drive
Bloomington, IN 47403
www.iuniverse.com
1-800-Authors (1-800-288-4677)

Because of the dynamic nature of the Internet, any Web addresses or links contained in this book may have changed since publication and may no longer be valid. The views expressed in this work are solely those of the author and do not necessarily reflect the views of the publisher, and the publisher hereby disclaims any responsibility for them.

ISBN: 978-1-4401-4033-4 (pbk)
ISBN: 978-1-4401-4034-1 (ebk)

Library of Congress Control Number: 2009927157

Printed in the United States of America

iUniverse rev. date: 5/29/2009

A Special Note Of Thanks:

To my husband

Gene Kruczek

for his support, patience, and encouragement

during the process of writing this text.

And

To my father's lifelong "brothers" in friendship,

Augie Sousa, **Saul Vinokur**, and **Joel Palmer**,

for providing anecdotes regarding

The Mount Vernon Boys Club

And

Memories of Life as Musicians.

"Dear Brother Phil,

You are just like music.

You spread good cheer with the beautiful beat of your heart.

You have that great spirit of humor combined
with your musical genius.

Whenever I think of you or see you, it lifts my spirit.

You are a class act all the way.

Thank you for allowing me to share part of your life."

Augie Sousa

For My Parents

Philip and Mary Curto Lucchine

Who Have Graced This Earth With

Style, Dignity, Purpose, Determination, Respect,

Generosity, Humor, Tradition, Honesty, Pride, Kindness,

And For

Their Gifts Of

Memories, Music, And Love.

"Music

Gives A Soul To The Universe,

Wings To The Mind,

Flight To The Imagination,

And

Life To Everything."

Plato

1

Independence Day

1981

Morning seemed hours overdue. Thick, ominous thunderheads blanketed the sky prolonging darkness and threatening the sun's arrival. I was exhausted having tossed my way through the night. Why was I so restless? And why on this steamy July morning was I shivering in a cold sweat? I had waited for this day for so long, yet rather than feelings of anticipation and excitation, I felt anxious and unsure; unnerved by the prospect of allowing another being into my private inner circle of three. In the depths of my soul I contemplated the commitment that would be absolute and for the rest of time. Squirming to alleviate the kink in my neck and pangs in the small of my back, I pondered the turns of the new directions my life would take and gasped for breath. Could I live with the life-altering situation I was getting myself into? Would I be happy with my new life style? After all, as an only child two months into my thirty-sixth year, I was independent and self-sufficient. One question after another popped into my head. I started to perspire and then to cry. Where *was* the morning sun? And *why* was it now raining on my special day?

My thoughts were suddenly interrupted by footsteps milling about the kitchen. The refrigerator door squeaked open, then with a thud smacked into the adjoining cabinet as it usually did when left unattended and allowed its limited range of motion. The bottles and jars on the ice box door smashed into each other as the door and the cabinet made contact causing a colossal crackle as though the entire row of glass had shattered into fragments. I could not help but discern the containers scraping the shelves as a shuffling and removal of the breakfast foods took place, but it was not until I detected the rush of water into the coffee pot that I was assured morning was finally upon me.

"Keep quiet!" Mom challenged dad who was busy counting the scoops of coffee he was measuring then pouring into the strainer section of the device. "You'll wake up Bobbi!"

"Wake up Bobbi?" he questioned loudly enough for me to hear. "If I know my daughter, she's up already!"

How right he was. How right he always was. No one knew me better. Ours was a rare and unique relationship. Without a word between us, each knew what the other was thinking. Often times we would laugh for seemingly no reason – no reason, that is, to whomever may have been around at the time and wondered what we were laughing at. It just seemed as though we were invariably on the same wavelength. We saw life through one set of eyes. It was uncanny.

I knew that within minutes dad would be leaning over the gold velvet, plastic covered couch where I laid curled in the fetal position on my left side waiting for the usual signal to rise and shine. As the clock wound down, a faint tapping sound alerted me to the approaching footsteps. With an exaggerated gait – knees nearly hitting his chin – dad tip-toed into the room looking as though he was part of a Laurel and Hardy out-take. That never failed to make me giggle, and he knew it. This morning the exaggeration was at its peak. Smiling, I hastened to close my eyes pretending to be asleep.

"Wanna cup a coffee?" dad whispered softly seemingly not wanting to frighten me out of a deep sleep yet knowing full well I was wide awake.

I opened my right eye, and as though that were the cue, dad hit me with a pillow. The pillow bounced off my noggin several more times.

"Ma!" I yelled calling for my mother to rescue me as she inevitably did. "Yurtz is hitting me!"

Yurtz was the name I had given my dad when I was a toddler, and, as far as I or anyone else knew, I created the name and the spelling of it. To me, the name was one of affection – endearment. The name became our secret code – our special link – a tight bond that formed between us. And, it was a name that only I could vocalize. I became so possessive that it would infuriate me to hear anyone else call him that. God forbid! After all, it was **my** special name for **my** dad, **my** confidant, **my** best friend, **my** hero.

"Will you leave Bobbi alone, and let her sleep!" Mom commanded from two rooms away.

"Sleep?" Yurtz hit me with the pillow again. "Sleep? Bobbi's up already!" he assured her as the pillow clunked me yet another time. "I told you she was up!"

This time I grabbed a hold of the pillow. Realizing I would now be able to retaliate, Yurtz quickly dashed from the scene.

"What time is it anyway?" I inquired as I wiped away the water and grains of sand from the corners of my eyes.

"Five thirty," Mom pointed out.

"Five thirty?" I yawned.

"Yes, it's only five thirty. Your father and I will be quiet so you can sleep for another hour," she promised.

Sleep another hour? I had not slept in several, and I certainly did not need additional time to toss – to turn – to think – to question.

The fragrance of freshly brewed coffee now permeated the air and aroused my senses. Yes, it was early, but it would be a busy day, and we all needed a head start. Breakfast was delicious, and 'va bene' was definitely in order. Everything was prepared just the way I liked it. The bacon, which was burnt so as to nearly be unrecognizable, formed a sharp contrasting arc around the sunny side part of the eggs. For a moment it reminded me of the contrasting feelings I was having about this day. The yolks beckoned me to poke my fork into them allowing the fluid, yellow interior to ooze out on to the toast. With his comical rendition of the Italian gesture – his four fingers delicately touching the thumb and the entire cupped hand motioning back and forth towards then away from his mouth – Yurtz enticed me to eat. "Mangia! Mangia! Va bene! Va bene!"

"Um, hum!" I agreed signaling my approval with the same cupped hand orientation this time fingers to my lips throwing the Italian kiss his way. "Tutto va bene!"

With so much to do the morning moved swiftly by. Neighbors dropped in to congratulate me, and I found myself in tears with each new well wisher. My eyes, red and swollen, had bags beneath that stretched to my chin line. As I squinted at my worn reflection in the foot wide mirror that separated the two living room windows in our apartment at 114 Valentine Street, I worried that my makeup would not be sufficient to cover the uncertainty on my face.

The rain continued with severity throughout the morning. As I gazed out of our third floor window, I caught a glimpse of my Aunt Nancy in the hallway of the Ninth Avenue apartment directly caddy-corner across the street. As she stepped onto the sidewalk to survey the massive black cloud cover, a thunderous assault erupted yet again. Taking her by surprise, she tripped backwards into the lobby. Peeking out from her safe vantage point, Aunt Nancy spotted me peering out the window, and her enthusiasm, which had been falling as fast as the raindrops, suddenly perked. The streamers and signs that were intended to adorn the white Cadillac I was to ride in on what was to have been a gloriously sunny day were made apparent, and despite the gloomy conditions, Aunt Nancy was determined to spread a little sunshine of her own. She frantically waved the multicolored ribbons as though she was a cheerleader whose team suffered another loss, and although her good intentions of spreading much desired illumination into the morning sparked about as much life into the day as a handful of limp noodles, I appreciated her effort to cheer me up.

"It's good luck!" Mom's younger sister shouted as she poked her head out of the doorway and pointed to the rain. "Rain brings good luck!" she reiterated to assure that I had heard her Italian myth.

Oh, my, I thought as the intensity of the rain increased. *If I need all this luck, I must surely be in big trouble!*

My mother's voice interrupted my train of thought. "Rosemarie's here!"

Rosemarie, our neighbor's daughter, had come to help me prepare. I had not seen her since we were teenagers – some twenty or twenty-five years perhaps – but with her flowing brunette hair, slender frame, and enormous blue eyes and deep-set dimples that dominated her face, she was as beautiful as I remembered her to be. We embraced like lost sisters reunited; neither one of us believing the other was really there.

"Can't believe it!"

"Me neither! It's so great to see you!"

"You look wonderful!"

"So do you!"

"How've you been?"

"Terrific. How 'bout you?"

"Great. It's been so long."

"Too long."

"This is so exciting!"

The conversation bounced back and forth in rapid succession like the ball going cross-court at Wimbledon on this very day. For a while I forgot about the rain – the misgivings – the commitment.

"O.K. you two," Mom intervened. "I just checked the kitchen clock, and I think it's time to get ready," she proposed as she handed Rosemarie the garment bag that protected and still concealed its contents.

As she removed the flowing white gown from its covering, Rosemarie gasped and her eyes sparkled with approval of what was revealed. The gown made of silk organza featured a high neckline of English net, bishop sleeves, and a ruffled skirt highlighted by silk Venice lace and pearls. A waltz-length mantilla double edged with lace and held by a cap covered with matching lace and pearls enhanced the whole ensemble.

"We have to be very, very careful not to get your makeup on the gown," Rosemarie insisted emphasizing the 'very'. She maneuvered her arms under the hemline of the dress and meticulously opened the bodice – then the neck.

"Put your arms straight overhead. I'll hold the gown above you and slip it down over your head."

Rosemarie hoisted herself onto the step stool, and reigning down on me from the top step, continued her commands. "Now don't move an inch – not an inch."

With a delicate yet swift and precise motion, Rosemarie slipped the gown overhead carefully preserving its purity. She buttoned the back and fluffed out the layers of crinolines that allowed the gown to billow out with soft, flowing lines.

"Oh, wow!" Rosemarie exclaimed as she wiped away the tears that enhanced her already notable facial features. "You look stunning! Absolutely stunning!"

"Smile!" directed Yurtz who was behind the movie camera acting like Cecil B. DeMile's Italian counterpart.

"Smile!" echoed an unfamiliar voice. When I turned out of curiosity in the direction of the voice, a flash of light struck my eyes and temporarily blurred my vision. As the colored dots before me faded, the photographer came into focus.

"Now, Mary," the photographer directed. "You and your daughter stand at the mirror."

As we took our assigned positions in front of the double dresser mirror and smiled at each other's reflection, I was entranced by the woman before me. I recalled the multitudes of photographs of Mom in her younger days while on tour with Yurtz. As a child I stared at those images sometimes for hours - her eyes mesmerizing - her beauty hypnotic. Some forty years had passed, and yet, she looked as glamorous as she did in the 1940's, not having lost one iota of those same qualities that Yurtz had fallen in love with and those that I often wished I had had. Elegantly garbed in a mauve, floor length ensemble with matching flowers in her hair, not even this bride could compare. Mom's radiance illuminated the pride and jubilation emanating from every pore. This was the happiest day of her life as she was about to have the son she had so desperately wanted.

The picture taker who was still in director mode rudely snapped me out of my trance.

"Smile, ladies!"

Snap/Flash!

"Now, Mary. Act as though you are combing Bobbi's hair."

Snap/Flash!

"Terrific. O.K., Mary. Pretend to button the gown. And smile!"

Snap/Flash!

"Mary. Hold the lipstick tube near Bobbi's lips."

Snap/Flash!

"Bobbi. Pin the corsage on your mother."

Snap/Flash!

"Now give each other a big hug and kiss!"

Snap/Flash!   Snap/Flash!   Snap/Flash!

"That's it!" the photographer blurted out nodding his approval with yet another snap/flash of his camera. "The natural shots are the best!"

But what was so natural about all of these poses? I questioned myself. For one thing, each new facet of the preparation was carefully orchestrated before being captured on film. And, how could anyone be 'natural' dressed such that sitting was next to impossible. I had the distinct feeling that I would spend the rest of the day standing and smiling – naturally, of course – until I collapsed.

With our departure for church a mere one hour away, my cousin and maid of honor, Toni, arrived just in time to join us in the next series of 'natural' photographs. Toni radiated in her tailored style gown of shimmering turquoise – a color highly complimentary to her olive complexion and deep brown hair and eyes. She was definitely the quintessential Italian beauty.

The photo session continued, but amidst the excitement and confusion, it suddenly occurred to me that one voice had become strangely quiet.

"Where's Yurtz?" I inquired scanning the bedroom then the living room where Mom, Toni, and I posed in front of the perfect backdrop – the ceiling to floor gold drapes.

"Yurtz!" I called several times before I proceeded to his favorite hangout where, in the recesses of his mind, he could easily escape to his private domain for hours on end. There he stood alone in the kitchen looking out of the window - his back facing me.

"There you are!" I quipped. There was no response. Having seen him this way many times, I knew he was in a daze in his own little world of thought. "Yurtz!" I called startling him back to reality.

"Yea", he acknowledged as he turned to face me.

"Where have you been?" I questioned.

Expecting his standard reply to that question, I was not at all surprised to hear him answer, "I went ice skating!"

The photographer had followed me and was snapping candid photos of the two of us. We ignored him.

"Don't you wanna take a picture with your favorite daughter?" I teased.

"You mean my **only** daughter," he sighed stressing the only.

Yurtz approached me – our eyes focused on each other. I knew the look in those eyes better than anyone else. The water was welling up like a stream about to overflow its banks after a heavy rainstorm such as the one this day.

Yurtz inhaled a huge supply of air. "Did you hear the one about the Heck-Ow-Wee Tribe?" he interjected trying to alleviate the tension with one of his famous jokes. He was a master at bantering, and as corny as the jokes may have been, they came to life as did he whenever he cracked one. It was all in the delivery – impeccable timing no doubt stemming from the innate internal rhythms projecting forth from the consummate musician to the royal jester. This accompanied by the priceless variety of facial expressions made for a belly laughing experience that would have made the best of the comedians fall over themselves. Invariably, I was his best audience quaking with hilarity at the unfolding of each tale to its concluding punch line - but not this time. The attempt at levity plunged like a lead balloon, and the ever jocular funnyman floundered for that which would bring both of us back from the depths.

"The other day I called the office of Schwartz, Schwartz, Schwartz, Schwartz, and Schwartz."

But this day, even one of my favorite anecdotes failed to arouse a positive response.

Simultaneously we inhaled consuming the entire supply of air within the room. With the lack of oxygen available for subsequent breaths, I felt faint in the vacuum that had been produced. The unusual conditions overtook our emotions and enabled us to hold back the deluge for the time being – but only for the time being. We knew the dam would break sometime this day for the both of us.

2

Birth Of The Blues

1917

Nothing could ever have prepared me for the events at hand. In disbelief and seemingly in another dimension of time and reality, I stood behind the man who, merely sixteen years earlier, proudly and briskly escorted me down the isle on that memorable fourth of July day, but who now before me was struggling to lift himself out of his wheelchair. The six broken ribs and punctured lungs from a car accident triggered a stroke, a blood clot in one leg, and several bouts of pneumonia complicated with asthmatic attacks. After months of agony and reoccurring trips to the hospital and a rehabilitation center, it was apparent to me that my father wanted to give up the fight.

My hero cannot lose this battle, I thought, and as I stood there forcing back the tears, I prayed this was just a nightmare stemming from some unknown, undigested food. But the twisting knots in my stomach only worsened as I stared down the foreboding, sterile hallway. I felt as though I was hanging from a cable car with the bottom having fallen out. The only isle I wanted to remember had a marble pillared walkway flanked by chestnut walls and multicolored stained glass windows. In all its splendor and ornate magnificence, the one hundred year old Church of Our Lady of Mount Carmel perched nobly on First Street in Mount Vernon, New York rivaled the great cathedrals of the world.

This new and unfamiliar isle was anything but that. Even the beauty of its name, *Rolling Hills*, could not mask the helplessness of its residents and of my father.

One therapeutic specialist and two aides strategically positioned themselves – one on either side of Yurtz and one behind the wheelchair. As I looked up for divine intercession, the memory of Mount Carmel's hand painted ceiling murals depicting the powers beyond suddenly blurred to nothing more than stark white; reminding me of the bleakness of this situation.

"You can do it, Philip," encouraged the therapist to his right. "We're here to help you."

Yurtz, exhausted from his unsuccessful attempts to rise, slumped over in his wheelchair. With his eyes glued to the floor as though mesmerized by the tiles, he shook his head – *no*.

"No is not an option. On the count of three, we're going to help lift you up," the therapist continued ignoring his negative response. "And", she added with assurance, "you're not only going to stand, but you're also going to walk today, Philip. Ready?"

Once again he shook his head – *no*. And once again ignoring this gesture, the count down began. With each number being slowly and deliberately stretched out, the count of "one" seemed to take as much time as counting to one hundred.

"Twooooooooooooooooooooooo."

Pulling up firmly from under his arms, both aides tugged on "three!"

Yurtz remained fixed in his chair.

"Let's try it again," she insisted. "This time, Philip, help us help you. Push up with those muscular legs of yours."

No.

"Come on now. You can do this," she persisted. "One – Two – Three!"

This time the firm tug was replaced by an even firmer yank.

"NOOOOOOOOOOOOOO!" Yurtz screamed sending a bone chilling vibration through my body that made me lunge forward to rescue him. The six-inch lift was aborted as Yurtz fell back into his seat.

"That's my **BAD ARM**!" he shrieked in writhing pain. "You're hurting my **BAD ARM**!"

The term 'bad arm' was Yurtz's way of referring to his paralyzed left arm, a paralysis not due to his stroke but rather of a life long physical affliction with childhood polio.

Born on February 8, 1917 to Italian immigrants Felice and Anna Maria (Petti) Lucchini of Casalciprano, Italy, Yurtz was the youngest of ten children officially on record as having been born. No one really knew how many actual offspring were born into the family, but according to stories, four sons died and the next four named in their honor. Whether that is fact or fiction, Yurtz was definitely the last of the children and his survival a miracle in itself.

The main birthing manager was midwife and close family friend, Mrs. Romanto, who single-handedly supervised the proceedings with a precision even the medical professionals would have been in awe of. Commandeered to assist in the birth and much to her displeasure, Helen, the oldest sibling in her twenties at the time, had to cancel her plans to attend a much anticipated dance – a sacrifice she never let her youngest brother forget but one which ultimately helped save his life.

The home birth itself went smoothly, and the baby boy was named Felice after his father and cherished namesake. But something was wrong – very wrong. Little Felice was in trouble. The blue tint of the new baby's shriveled skin deepened as difficulty in breathing became increasingly more evident. In the early 1900's many babies so afflicted did not survive infancy. Several babies had already succumbed in this family previous to Felice, and the thought of losing another was unbearable.

The prognosis was bleak at best. Baby Felice labored to breathe and was barely clinging to life. With tears streaming down her reddened cheeks, Helen gave up hope for her new baby brother. She had gone through this situation before, recognized the signs, and was certain of the outcome.

But Mrs. Romanto, the pillar of fortitude and unyielding determination, remained comparatively calm as she quickly improvised then set in motion a plan – a course of action so unimaginable, so bizarre that in today's eye would be viewed as grounds for child abuse.

"Riscaldare il forno!" Romanto commanded. "Riscaldare il forno!"

Startled, Helen's forehead wrinkled in an attempt to make sense out of what she thought she had heard. *Riscaldare il forno? Heat up the oven? Heat up the oven? The oven? What is Mrs. Romanto thinking? The oven? What insane plan could this be?* Helen froze.

While Helen stood affixed, time and Mrs. Romanto seemed to be moving at the speed of light. A life was hanging in the balance, and this was no time for mutiny.

With clinched fists, Mrs. Romanto threw up her arms evermore forcefully. Controlled but with complete dominance, she bellowed, "Riscaldare il forno!" The words echoed off the bedroom walls – "Riscaldare il forno!"

Helen and her father, Pop, scurried feverously complying with every Romanto order as though GI's responding to their sergeant. She was in attack mode and in complete charge in the battle for life.

Mrs. Romanto cocooned Felice in blankets and hurriedly made her way to the kitchen. She signaled Helen to open the oven door. Much to Helen and Pop's disbelief, Mrs. Romanto gently placed Felice on top of the warmed oven door panel! The vigil ensued.

Throughout the night, Mrs. Romanto and Helen took turns praying over and monitoring baby Felice as he lay there helplessly on the opened oven door. Pop joined Mamma in the bedroom and together prayed to Saint Joseph. The pain of witnessing the baby's fight for life was overwhelming as each hour struggled to turn to the next. Exhaustion prevailed – but so did the vigil.

Whether it was the warmth, the prayers, or both, the second morning found the new born responding. As Felice's breathing hastened, his shriveled skin dramatically chameleoned from blue to flesh pink. Problems with breathing and with asthma would haunt Felice throughout his life, nearly taking it several times. But this time he beat the odds. Pop and Mamma thanked Saint Joseph for the miracle of their new little boy.

It is unclear when or how the paralysis set in, but it occurred suddenly. Yurtz vaguely recalled falling from a slide onto his shoulder, but doctors, unable to detect any broken bones or other serious injuries, diagnosed the condition as childhood polio, a crippling and potentially deadly disease. Many so afflicted were confined to *iron lungs* for the remainder of their short lives, and thousands of young lives were altered forever by an ailment for which there would not be a vaccine until 1953.

Mamma, a 4' 10" power-packed matriarch wearing her characteristic smock and apron was determined to bring life back to Felice's dead arm. Without available remedies, she engaged her own potion – the ultimate meat tenderizer – olive oil! For several hours each day, she lubricated her son's arm with olive oil, and as though kneading dough for the homemade breads, macaroni, and biscotti she was famous for, gently massaged the arm as she prayed for signs of movement.

"For hours at a time my mother would rub my arm with olive oil," Yurtz vividly remembered. "Then my sisters and brothers would take turns rubbing the olive oil while my mother prayed to Saint Joseph for help in bringing life to my arm."

After each treatment, Felice's arm was placed in a sling for protection until the next day – the next treatment. Mamma's devotion was endless as this ritual continued up to Felice's pre-teens. But the arm remained motionless. Neither oil treatments nor prayers were enough to create a second miracle.

3

A Rebirth

Late 1920's

Mamma sheltered her little boy for all good reasons, yet how was she to know or to comprehend the impact of this on Felice throughout his life. The preoccupation and attention given to his paralyzed arm produced a reticent, easily intimidated, non-aggressive young boy whose lack of confidence and low self-esteem escalated with age and ultimately hindered his pursuit of dreams.

For nearly ten years Felice watched life from the sidelines while the world seemed to be spinning by him. Then it happened – a profound change in events that enabled the merry-go-round to finally slow up enough for Felice to jump on to it.

The life changing event occurred at the Tenth Avenue Boys Club of Mount Vernon, New York. The Boys Club grew out of a need to keep the local kids off the streets and out of trouble, and in 1912 the first Club sprang up in a make-shift church gymnasium in the Martens' building at 16 East First Street. Forty or so first attendees blossomed into hundreds of boys chomping at the bit for activity. As the attendance sky-rocketed, the facility became quickly cramped then over-stuffed. With at least three different changes in the Club location throughout the City of Mount Vernon, the Club finally found its permanent home at 45 North Tenth Avenue.

The year was 1920. The thirteen room building, known as the Varian House, was purchased through donations and fund raisers and allowed for multiple activities to be held in varying parts of the Club house. In the 1920's records indicated that yearly attendance rose to 20,000, as Club members flocked to the house on a nightly basis. In May of 1925 a forty foot by seventy foot gymnasium was added to the structure. The fully equipped addition not only had bleachers which could easily seat five hundred spectators, it boasted a shower room and a stage for show productions. Sill in operation nearly ninety years since it first opened its doors, the Club house is surrounded by single family homes in the center of a residential block. The house became the center of a new life for Felice.

Buddy Augie Sousa urged Felice to accompany him to the Club. Felice's understandable reluctance gave way to acceptance at the continued prodding. Felice and Augie met in the middle of Mount Vernon Avenue between the blocks of Bond and Bleeker Streets. The hometown grocery store which sat there was a comfortable place to start as it was owned by Felice's parents until they lost the business giving away food during the Great Depression.

The five city block trek to the Club seemed like an eternity as the anticipation of arrival mounted. The gym was bursting at the seams with kids, and the sweet sounds of laughter coming from the basketball court brought a smile to Felice's face. Felice hurriedly plopped on the bleachers hoping not to draw attention to himself. Although enjoying the action from this vantage point, Felice secretly and desperately wanted to play too. But the teams had already been chosen and the games underway he rationalized. Anyway, he was certain he would never be selected, so he might just as well be content to savor the moments as they were.

Everyday for nearly two weeks the routine remained the same – but not this day. An ear-piercing whistle resounded in the gym bringing the games to a screeching halt. In the middle of the gym floor stood a new leader – one of imposing stature – Coach Gorman. Signaling the boys with a sweeping motion of both arms, the boys surrounded him. From his seat Felice was hard-pressed to hear what was being said, but it must have been important as the boys listened intently to every word.

Coach Gorman raced up and down the court coaching, refereeing, and encouraging all at the same time, and it was during one of his laps that he noticed the boy sitting by himself on the bleachers.

"Hey, son!" Coach Gorman hollered pointing in the direction where Felice sat.

Felice turned to see if someone was seated behind him and was surprised to see no one there.

"Yes! You over there, son!" the coach bellowed so loudly that all activity ceased immediately, each boy thinking he had done something wrong. "What are you doing way over there, son?" he rhetorically questioned.

Waving Felice over and finger pointing to a spot on the gym floor, Coach Gorman demanded, "Come over here, son, and stand on this line."

Always mindful of respecting his elders, Felice did as he was told.

"What's your name, son?" the coach inquired.

Bowing his head in submission, Felice quietly muttered, "Philip, sir."

Several years prior, Felice had changed his own name not to dishonor his beloved father but for his own sanity. The change occurred during the first day of school roll call. "Felice?" the teacher called. "Here," came a faint whisper from the back of the room. Not having heard the acknowledgement, the teacher re-questioned, "Felice?" Once again, the soft voice in the rear of the classroom was not distinguishable for the teacher stretching forward to hear a reply. Frustrated by the lack of response, the teacher gave it one last and final attempt. "Felice? Is **she** here? Felice? Is **she** here?" 'She? She? She?' echoed in Felice's head as everyone in the class laughed at his expense. From that day forward, Felice christened himself Philip!

"What's the sling for, Philip?" Coach Gorman inquired.

"It holds my bad arm," Philip explained wishing he were anywhere but there at that moment.

The gym had become so painfully quiet that a pin dropping would have sounded like the fireworks exploding on my Fourth of July wedding day.

"Is it broken, Philip?" the coach interrogated.

"No, sir!" Philip divulged.

"Well, then, what's the problem, son?" The inquisition continued with all the boys eaves-dropping on this now community conversation.

"I can't move it." Philip revealed while lowering his head in complete embarrassment.

"And it's not broken?" a puzzled coach repeated as he squinted at the sling attempting to make sense of it.

Squirming from all of the unwanted attention about his arm, Philip murmured, "It's paralyzed. My arm is paralyzed!"

During that time there were four boys at the Club afflicted with polio. Philip and Gino had the same one arm condition and both wore 'slings'. Frank had one leg affected while Sidney's both legs remained motionless requiring him to use crutches. Coach Gorman, a superior gymnast, swimmer, and high diver, once toured the East Coast with Johnny Weissmuller of Tarzan fame giving high diving exhibitions, and he was not about to allow any of 'his boys' back away from challenges. "The four young boys were an inspiration to all of us," wrote Augie, "and Mr. G. was there to show all of us what the human being is capable of with guidance from others and their own personal effort."

"O.K., then, son! You seem to be a brave young man, Philip" the coach reassured as he rescued Philip from the pit he had sunken in to. But just as Philip was about to breathe a sigh of relief, he heard the unthinkable – the unimaginable. Coach Gorman went for the jugular!

"Now, son. Take off that sling and get in the game!"

"But………………"

"Well, since your arm is not broken," the coach interrupted before the pleading could begin, "there shouldn't be a problem removing that sling – should there?"

Panic overwhelmed Philip. "But my Mamma told me never to take it off –NEVER!"

Unwavering and totally determined, Coach Gorman promised, "As soon as I leave here tonight, I will talk to your Mamma, Philip."

What? Philip thought. *Coach Gorman will challenge the world's highest authority – Mamma Lucchini? He must be crazy! Mamma will surely go after him with that dreaded wooden spoon!"* Philip's mind and heart were racing out of control.

"Go ahead now, young man, take off that sling!"

All eyes were glued on Philip. Under the crushing pressure that was suffocating him, Philip began his slow decent into hell. His right hand pulled the fabric over his head until it rested on his left shoulder. Even through the unbearable heaviness in the gym, the vibrations of Philip's thumping heart could be felt by all. Philip hesitated what seemed to be eternity garnering the courage to finalize his death. Lowering his head to hide the tears that were streaming down his cheeks, Philip slid the cloth off the rest of the way. The sling was off! Finally off! Philip's arm fell with a thud and dangled limp at his side. But the sling was off!

"Yes!" proclaimed Coach Gorman with an approving smile that cut through the tension. "Now I know you are a brave young man!"

Much to Philip's astonishment, the boys instantaneously erupted in cheers for their new teammate. "The North Side and the West Side boys were a bunch of good guys," Philip recalled. "When they chose sides, they all wanted me. And NO ONE EVER MADE FUN OF MY ARM!" A glow came over Philip's reddened face as the burden of ten years lifted with the removal of that which tied him down for so long.

"O.K. everyone. Back to your positions, and let's get the games underway!" the coach shouted acting as though what had just transpired was no big deal. No big deal? Maybe not to the coach, but to Philip

....

The boys scurried to their areas, but unsure of his position, Philip remained fixed on the line attempting to decipher the implications of what had just transpired.

The whistle blew.

"Now, son, take it in play!"

With those instructions, Coach Gorman turned abruptly and snapped the ball. Before he could scarcely catch his thoughts or his breath, Philip felt the ball hit his gut. Instinctively, his right arm surrounded the ball, and Philip beamed with pride at having made the one-arm catch. Coach Gorman winked then nodded for Philip to take the ball on to the court. Philip complied and even surprised himself at how naturally he began to dribble the ball.

That afternoon Philip did not make one basket, but that did not matter. The sling was off – finally off. And Philip was playing ball – finally playing. So powerful a day and so indelibly etched in his mind, Philip recounted the impact of that day often, and over seventy years later, proclaimed, "**THAT WAS THE DAY I WAS BORN!**"

4

It's All In The Game

With Philip's rebirth, a new sense of freedom emerged from hibernation. The cocoon shed, Philip's natural athletic abilities took flight, even to the point of him becoming "an excellent tumbler at the Club." Soaring to heights that astounded on-lookers, Philip even surprised himself. But Coach Gorman took it in stride and was delighted at his new recruit and star player.

In a game where two hands ruled, Philip's one-handed shots became legendary. This unique technique had never been used or seen before. "He would cradle the ball in his left palm, pass it to the right hand, and then shoot. He was a pioneer and participated on teams and in leagues." Philip was not trying to be inventive, he was merely playing the only way he knew how – the only way he could. Pal Augie Sousa declared that in 1929 Philip was "the first one-handed shooter" he had ever seen and that "his hook shot was deadly!" The 'one-arm wonder' and his famous hook shots became widely known on the basketball courts throughout the neighboring towns. Philip was amazed by the notoriety. All he ever wanted to do was to play.

And play he did - game after game - basket after basket - win after win. The endless hours of practice were finally reaping rewards. But there was never any time to revel in the last victory. Each victory brought the team closer to the game of a lifetime. Excitement mounted at the realization that a Boy's Club championship was in grasp. The showdown was set.

Coach Gorman knew his boys were ready. The North Side boys had come too far to let this one get away. A rally pep talk and the team took to the court in their usual fashion. Wearing whatever individual tee shirts and shorts they could muster up, the group hardly appeared like an organized bunch. Nothing matched. With times tough and money hard to come by, uniforms were out of the question. Each boy wore whatever his family could afford. Disheveled, the group resembled the 'Our Gang' comedy kids. The slip-shod group would have been the laughing stock of the basketball community had it not been for their winning record. Regardless of their comedic appearance, the boys felt confident and ready to take on the toughest of opponents – the defending champions.

Stomach butterflies increased in size and number anticipating the arrival of the other team. Gathering the jittery group together, Coach Gorman gave a rousing speech instilling team pride. "Play your game, boys! Play like you've played all season, and………."

Just then the gym erupted and the rafters shook as the three time champs took to the court. The North Side boys stood motionless and in silence as though collectively hypnotized. *Uniforms? Were they really wearing uniforms?* Each boy rubbed his eyes as if to wipe away the mirage before him. Yes, *they were in uniforms* – perfect uniforms from head to foot! Reality hit like a brick. There was no denying that they certainly looked like champions in their perfect uniforms. Philip looked down on his outfit and felt nauseous. *Are they as good as they look? If they play the way they look*, Philip thought…….. The knot in Philip's stomach twisted ever-tighter cutting off all circulation. He felt his legs buckle.

Going through a myriad of complex drills out on the court, the opposition, once thought to have been in the same Club league, suddenly took on the look of the NBA All-Stars. So smooth – so polished. The North Side boys gawked in awe. It seemed as though the gym walls were caving in around them. The intimidation factor kicked in as each guy contemplated the inevitable annihilation of the team. They were doomed, and they knew it.

The whistle blew.

What had been an animated group of hopefuls just ten minutes prior to game time reverted to a group of down-troddens shuffling out onto the floor. Uncertainty and self-pity screamed back at the fans. But Coach Gorman would have none of it and refused to have his team give up before they even started. His deafening voice pierced the eardrums of the spectators – "Play *your* game, boys! Play *your* game!"

That may have been easier said than done. The first few minutes dragged to eternity. The North Side boys were unraveled and sinking into the quicksand that anchored their feet. They were already down by four buckets and being consumed at the speed of sound as the other team swished basket after basket. The whistle blew as time-out was called. Coach Gorman's exuberance and confidence never wavered as he re-grouped the team's mind-set.

As though lightning had sent a jolt of electricity directly into the team's psyche, Gorman's boys snapped out of their trance. They bolted back to the heat of the battle with aggression and intent. The pace of the game escalated, as did the team's output. The half ended with the score tied.

The encounter continued. The North Side boys were in sync and in control with basket after basket. Four buckets in a row for the 'one-arm wonder' gave the North Side team a commanding lead. The crowd was on its feet. Philip's rhythm and dead eye accuracy seemed unstoppable. The opposition was desperate.

A North Side team member grabbed the jump ball in mid-air. With the ball having been hurled to him, Philip made his way up the court. Launching the ball towards the net for yet another two-pointer, Philip suddenly felt a crunching blow. Three opponents sandwiched Philip plunging him to the floor and landing full force on top of him. The thud echoed in the gym. As the three culprits lifted themselves from Philip's crushed body, the crowd booed and hissed their disapproval of the cheap shot and illegal football tackle.

Amid the commotion, Philip remained on the floor wrought in pain and clutching his ankle. Coach Gorman and the team surrounded Philip where he lay injured. The crowd silenced. What was first feared to have been a broken ankle turned out to be a rather severe sprain.

Swollen and unable to put pressure on his foot, Philip had to be removed from the rest of the game.

Sidelined with his ankle wrapped in ice and leg elevated, Philip sat on the bench with mixed emotions. Flashback after flashback popped into his head clouding then illuminating his thoughts with terrifying then exhilarating memories................***the sling***..........a childhood sidelined..........*the sling*..........desperate to play and to belong ....*the sling*..........the coach..........*no sling*..........liberation from captivity..........*no sling*..........life a new. Never could Philip have envisioned his elevation from the pit to the team wonder. A mystical aurora surrounded him.

At 5' 6" in shoes, Philip was certain his basketball days were numbered. He probably would have been right had it not been for Coach Gorman's recommendation to Edison Vocational and Technical High School's basketball Coach Logan. As a favor to Coach Gorman and much to Philip's surprise, Coach Logan requested that he try out for the high school team. Even more shocking was that Philip made second team varsity! Although Philip did not play much nor was he the star 'wonder' on the high school court, he was proud of his accomplishment at having made the team at all.

But Philip's regard for the Boys Club team could not be surpassed nor even equaled. The Boys Club had laid the foundation for a sense of fulfillment and gratitude that would forever change a young boy's life. Lifelong friendships became Philips's cornerstone, and he so often fondly affirmed, "The Boys Club was the best growing up I did!"

The Mount Vernon Boys Club allowed Philip to achieve that which seemed impossible and improbable for so many years. The championship game was just another game. But for Philip, it was more than that. Childhood years wrought with frustration and anguish dissipated on the court.

Nursing his injury on the sideline was icing on the cake. Philip admittedly reveled in the perception that "the only way to control me – was to hurt me!"

It couldn't get any better than that. But it did. The North Side boys claimed the title!

5

The Gifted

Although Philip was enjoying his athletic stint in basketball as well as in touch football where he "even ran for a touchdown", he knew that phase of his life would be short-lived. His less than athletic physical stature along with the physical challenges of a paralyzed left arm gave him no other option than to pursue a different course. A rush of rhythm brewed from within, and although Philip's heart raced with excitement on the basketball court, he gravitated towards his true calling as a musician – like his father and his father's father before that. The Lucchini family was a clan of musicians for as many past generations as history had recorded, and like those previous in his lineage, Philip had music circulating through his veins as part of his life's blood. The legacy was there all along waiting for him to embrace it.

In Italy, the Lucchinis were traveling musicians – all of them. And Philip was about to follow in their rhythmic footsteps and embark on his life's calling.

Philip's siblings were musically inclined as well – trumpeter Giovanni, pianist Pasquale, guitarist Andrew, and pianists Helen, Rose, Christine, and Josephine. All were vocalists as well. Rhythm was part of the nature of the Lucchini group. Christine won a dance contest, and all eight could have done likewise as each was capable of bringing down the house as tap and swing dancers.

But according to Philip, the most talented of all was their Pop, Felice. Although musically uneducated, Pop was a master maestro able to play and to teach every instrument, earning him the nickname 'Grandpa Toot-Toot' by his adoring grandchildren. Pop's extraordinary, versatile talent often times landed him in diametrically opposed sections of the Citizens Band Orchestra of Westchester County. In the same concert he would often be the principal clarinetist on one number and the principal sousaphone player on another. Exceptional on both sides of the orchestra, Pop could switch from the treble clef, reed instrument to the base clef, brass mouthpiece instrument as easily as switching a light bulb on and off. "Pop played a mad tuba!" Philip boasted often. "When he played *The William Tell Overture*, Pop blew me away with his tuba part. He was unrivaled. He was the greatest."

Philip's enlightenment occurred when he first heard his oldest brother, Johnny, playing trumpet in a local dance band. Totally captivated by the sound, Philip's propensity towards the horn became his choice of instrument.

Whether after school or after the Boys Club, Philip took a daily pilgrimage to Johnny and wife Katie's apartment, which was located a basketball throw away from the Bronx. There he began to hone his skills. But just holding the horn was a major challenge in itself. Because his paralyzed left arm was unable to hold the implement up, Philip improvised. While holding the trumpet in his right hand, he anchored the dead weight of his left arm onto the shaft of the instrument thus allowing his left fingers to reach the valves. This normal right hander then used his left fingers to press the valves; a grip and finger method completely opposite of how a normal right-handed trumpet player holds and fingers the instrument. Because his right arm had to bear the weight of the instrument as well as the dead weight of his left arm, the horn would often times point downward towards the floor rather than straight out parallel to it. Philip's trumpet posture may have been affected, but the sweet, melodious sounds he created were not.

Johnny realized Philip's potential early on. His commitment to daily practices was religious in nature and his raw talent superior to that of Johnny's. It was time for Johnny to let go, and he knew it.

"Hey, Philly!" Johnny greeted his youngest brother at the apartment door one afternoon. "Come on in." Johnny stepped aside so Philip could enter. "You've been coming here to practice for quite a while now, haven't you?"

"Yea!" Philip nodded then bowed his head in a show of gratitude. "And thanks for letting me borrow your horn everyday. I'm havin' fun!"

"I know you are," Johnny agreed. "But with school and all, it just takes too much time for you to come back and forth every day."

Philip acted quickly to clear up any misconceptions that Johnny may have had. "Oh, no. I don't mind at all. I can't wait to get here." With a tinge of trepidation of what he feared Johnny would say next, Philip continued before the axe could fall. "I love coming here to play! It's a blast!"

Something doesn't seem right. Why is Johnny even home at this hour? Philip pondered. Philly tried to assess the situation as fast as he could. *Maybe I shouldn't have used the word blast. Maybe the neighbors are complaining.*

"I won't blast anymore," Philip promised in a hurry to make amends. "I'm sorry if I upset the neighbors. I'll use the mutes and play more softly."

"Nobody's complaining!" Johnny chuckled. "In fact, the neighbors love it!"

"So, what's the problem?"

"There is no problem."

If there's no problem, Philip deliberated, *then what? Did I damage the horn? No! Yesterday when I placed the horn back in its case, it was in perfect condition.* Philly's mind mulled over countless speculations attempting to fit the pieces of this puzzle together. He needed comebacks for whatever problems may have arisen, but his mind went blank as he waited for the inevitable bad news.

"If you don't want me to come here anymore, how will I practice?" Philly fretted.

"You can practice at your own house." Johnny instructed.

"How?" Philly felt a rush of water welling in his eyes. With money as tight as it was for necessities, there was no way the family could even afford to buy him a team uniform, had the team had a uniform, let alone a trumpet. "How can I practice at home if I don't have a horn?"

"Well, now you do!" Johnny smiled as he presented Philip with the locked case containing his most treasured possession. "You have this one!"

Stunned, Philip stood motionless and temporarily speechless. "You mean – your horn?"

"Not any more, kid. It's now your horn. Play hard and make me proud!"

Philip could have slam-dunked a ball into a basketball net had the apparatus been available. He raced home in record time with his horn tucked safely under his right arm, swung open the back screen door, and howled loud enough for the entire West side of Mount Vernon to hear – "Mamma! Johnny gave me his horn!"

Although Mamma, later affectionately known as 'Grandma Toot-Toot', was excited for her baby boy, Pop was more difficult to convince of his son's desire. After all, Pop had taught all of his children, but none of them pursued music as seriously as he had hoped. He was certain little Philly would play a few years, become disenchanted, then put the horn aside as did the rest of his offspring. Besides, Pop wanted all of his children and now his youngest boy to learn classical – a genre that Philip clearly was not suited for.

One afternoon, Pop arrived home early from work catching Philip's daily practice session. Listening intently to the multitudes of notes blaring from the attic, Pop had the instant realization that if the *classics* were meant to be played *that* way, he would have no choice but to retire his tuba.

Hearing the back door close, Philip flew down the attic stairs.

"So, what do you think, Pop? How do I sound? How do I play?"

Any thought Philip may have had about dazzling his dad with jazz was quickly squelched as Pop gave his brutal assessment. "You – ah – play – ah – bull – ah – shit!"

Whether Pop was kidding or not, Philip took the comment to heart. He wanted his idol's approval in the worst way. And although jazz was never out of his realm during his faithful practices in the attic, little

Philip taught himself to read music and to play those classical pieces Pop would have approved of. Philip was ecstatic when Pop invited him to join the community band. To play in the same band as his hero, his Pop, was the ultimate experience. Philip was beside himself. Finally, he had the blessing of the most important person in his life.

6

Strike Up The Band

Early 1930's

A group of West Side Mount Vernon teen friends, all having talent and sharing the same passion for music, formed a band, and in 1932, the **Vernon Troubadours** were officially born. The original seven members included: Tommy Castelli (Drums), Joel Palmer (Piano), Tony Mongarelli (Guitar), Norman Kelly, Hank Kass, and Angelo Greco (Saxophones and Clarinets), and fifteen year old Philip Lucchine (Trumpet).

From the inception of the group, Philip knew that his career path had been set, and he quickly adopted the stage name Phil Keen - a take-off and shortened version of Lucchine. But Pal Augie Sousa had a different take. "The name 'Keen' fit Phil well," Augie assessed. "In the early days, 'Keen' was an expression that was used to describe a person who was held in high esteem because that person was outstanding in many positive ways. That was Phil 'Keen', all right!"

With one change and three additions, the group expanded to ten: Norman Kelly who opted not to travel was replaced by Bill Virga (Saxophone and Vocals), and Saul Vinokur (Saxophone), Joe Tanno (Bass), and Jimmy Dee (Vocalist) joined the group.

The majority of the guys attended A.B. Davis High School on the hill overlooking Gramatan Avenue while Phil, Tony, and Angelo were students at the newly opened Edison Vocational and Technical

High School on Third Avenue. Tommy, the elder statesman of the group by at least four years, had not graduated either school, but that never kept him from completing his rounds. Although not enrolled, Tommy strolled the hallowed halls of Edison Tech and announced the upcoming practice sessions with an authority that suggested he owned the building. There so often, it was assumed he belonged there; his presence never challenged.

Phil, Tony, Tommy, Angelo, and a few others started the very first Edison High School band under the direction of Carl E. Licht. During one session, Mr. Licht stopped the rehearsal, pointed to Tommy, and forcefully indicated that he needed to be more dramatic on the drums in one particular section of the music. "You've got to hit it with a ton of bricks!" he instructed hammering his fist on the music stand in front of him. "Got it, Tom?"

Tommy nodded indicating he fully understood the direction.

"Now, boys. Once again from the top. And Tommy," Mr. Licht challenged again, "hit it with a ton of bricks!"

When reaching the section in question, Tommy complied with the full force of a tornado. He whacked the set with such explosiveness the drum rolled right off the stage! With the rest of the band members choking not to laugh, Mr. Licht, having not skipped a beat, gave Tommy an ear-to-ear grin. "Now you've got it, son!"

This tale struck a chord with me. Mr. Licht, music teacher, eventually became Dr. Licht, Superintendent of Music for the Mount Vernon Public School System. It was in that capacity that we crossed paths. Dr. Licht instituted the revolutionary 'Youth Marches On' program wherein the best musicians from each school combined to form one gargantuan ensemble. The concert was held yearly in the massive auditorium at Washington Junior High School, and I always looked forward to my participation in this superb event on the grandest stage in the district. It had been some twenty-six years since my dad and Tommy's experience with Mr. Licht. His title may have changed from Mr. to Dr. but his enthusiasm and favorite rumblings never did. "Hit it like a ton of bricks" he commanded at our 'Youth Marches On' rehearsal. We complied but apparently not with Tommy's gusto. Our drums remained on stage.

The Mount Vernon School District had a music program second to none. There were seven or eight elementary schools, four junior highs, and two high schools crammed into a four square mile city just thirteen miles north of New York City and sandwiched between the Bronx and Yonkers. The music program in each school was equipped with talented music teachers, instruments for loan, and full band uniforms for every student. On the corner of High and Elm Streets sat Hamilton Elementary School. When the new building opened in 1945 the commitment to the music program was evident as the facility was equipped with a music room and a then state of the art sound proof practice room.

When Mount Vernon held its annual parade down the main shopping thoroughfare along Fourth Avenue through Gramatan Avenue, it was a spectacle of enormous proportions and one to behold. Throngs of humanity lined up all along the entire parade route cheering the passing marchers.

The two Grande Avenues were the locations of some of Westchester County's finest shops. The list endless, shopping was invariably a full day affair. Genungs, a three-story, up-scale department store, sporting the first escalator I had ever seen, towered at the center of the hub on Fourth Avenue. Elegantly appointed, it featured exclusive clothing and the finest of linens, jewelry, and household items. As a teenager I served in two luxurious departments – lingerie and jewelry. Nightgowns and undergarments including panties, bras, slips, and hosiery were neatly folded and contained in size and color labeled, clear drawers behind an oblong counter. Upon the request of the ladies of distinction, I would remove the entire drawer, place it on the counter, and show the latest fashions one item at a time. The strun-about method was not tolerated as managers continually patrolled the isles insuring the customer the highest degree of service, product, and neatness.

The fine jewelry section welcomed customers as they entered the front of the store. A circular, floor to countertop glass case revealed the glitz and glitter beckoning browsers and buyers. Although I adored my position at each station, I especially loved my post at the ornamental venue. Not owning even so much as one trinket, I delighted in donning my favorites from the massive collection. Each shift, I wore one, two, or three different pieces and felt like a debutant as I modeled my wares. Even for only a short while each evening, it was magical.

The Fair, a two-story home goods extravaganza dominated the opposite side of the street. Items purchased in the basement of The

Fair presented the customer with a primeval system of payment. At the register, the hand-written receipt and cash were placed in a small box. When the cashier rang the bell which was anchored to the counter, the assembly would be hoisted up to the main floor register. Within minutes, the box containing the stamped 'paid' receipt and the customer's change would be lowered to the basement floor which was reminiscent of the dumb-waiter system in our apartment.

A variety of family owned shops surrounded the two larger masters and summoned shopper from miles around. The streets bustled with activity as scores of buyers flooded the businesses: Fennell's Fine Furniture, Mimi's Exclusive Millinery, Popular Cotton, Treasure Island, Raymond Jewelers, Albert's Hosiery, Woolworth's Five and Dime, Dorothea Pharmacy, the Beehive Restaurant, and Fanny Farmer Chocolates thrived all along Fourth Avenue. Crossing over the bridge to Gramatan Avenue, a host of additional businesses lured shoppers: Proctor's Grand Movie Theatre, Barrish Stationary Store, Charlains Jewelry, The Gramatan Men's Shop, Broadbeck's Music Store, Pick-A-Package Confectioners, Bartletta's Florist, Artuso's Italian Bakery, and Duffy's Five and Ten, an all-inclusive shop filled to the rafters with every item ever produced to that time. Whatever it was that was wanted or needed and could not be found elsewhere in the whole of Westchester County was sure to be located somewhere amid the massive inventory at Duffy's. The seemingly chaotic placement of floor to ceiling overstuffed bins and shelves could have created a shopper's nightmare yet ultimately produced a delightful seek and search detective's experience. But even when the haystack seemed insurmountable, the owners and workers at Duffy's could escort the customer to the exact location of even a single needle. It was an amazing feat even by Houdini's standards.

On parade days, it was difficult to find a clearing anywhere along the six block route as on-lookers sought their viewing spots well in advance of the pageantry. Yurtz recalled his participation in Edison High School's very first parade. Saxophonist extraordinaire, Tony, who curiously boasted two nicknames, 'Monk' and 'Zum', took the helm as the drum major. He led the meager numbered band members through their paces, bedazzling the multitude with his strutting and baton twirling capabilities. Flipping the long shafted, bulbous end of his metal rod into the air high above the building rooftops, Monk caught the descending implement behind his back or between his legs. Crowds roared their approval at his amazing talent: Phil was in awe of it.

As the band proudly stepped forward in marching unison, the grand stand came into view. In an attempt to impress the town dignitaries sitting to their left, the band blasted forth sounding like a two-hundred piece unit. Monk hurled his baton into the atmosphere as all eyes followed it upward seemingly beyond the clouds. With the confidence of his successful previous catches, Monk reached behind his back for yet another show of remarkable mastery. Whether it was a sudden gust of wind or just plain misjudgment, the metal bar hit the pavement and rolled down the street with Monk in hot pursuit. The guys lost it. Laughing and unable to blow another note or drum another beat, the group broke ranks and raced to catch up to their leader; thus leaving the dignitaries wondering whether their monies had been well spent on this music venture.

With their marching days well behind them, the Vernon Troubadours concentrated on their true calling and began their entertainment days. Luckily, several guys had places where the fledgling group could practice. They gathered on South Street in Monk's garage during the summers and in Saul's basement at 8 Grove Street during the winters, never missing a beat no matter the season.

Even before the Troubadours ever officially performed, they had an audience. Washington School custodian Whitey Bach and his son Johnny sat outside on the lawn of whichever house the group practiced at and listened to every session. Whether it was Whitey's influence is unclear, but the group's first gig was to be held at Whitey's school. The teenagers sported what was affordable and up-to-date attire – black jackets, white trousers, and white buck shoes. Although there were variations in their long neck ties and socks, it was their music not their garb that mattered. The upbeat music blew the crowd on to the dance floor, resulting in the original one time gig becoming a long-standing one. Graduating to all black suits and cream color matching ties, the Vernon Troubadours performed every Thursday evening from 8-10:30 pm for the free dances at the Washington School. Bright-eyed teenagers packed the gym each week. The word was out.

7

Kiss It Goodbye

According to many, Phil Keen played in the stratosphere, several octaves higher than anyone else around at the time. "Hey! Come down to Earth, Philly!" the guys teased.

"I have to play it like I feel it," he protested. "And man, that's where I'm at!" Then back to the stratosphere he flew.

An event that profoundly changed Philip's musical life forever occurred innocently enough at the home of a friend. An afternoon barbecue spread lay before Philip's watering mouth, and he joyfully partook of a little of everything on his plate. While gnawing on a juicy spare rib, he bit the bone breaking his two upper front teeth. That evening, after testing a few notes on the horn and feeling as though all was well, he continued the gig full force, his notes soaring into outer space. But by the end of the set, something was frightfully wrong. Philip's upper lip had split wide open where the jagged-edged teeth pressed against his lip on the trumpet mouthpiece. *It'll be okay by tomorrow,* he hoped.

"Hey, Phil. There's blood on your lips," observed one of the band members.

Blood. Never before had that word delivered instantaneous blows of despair and ominous horror. Philip dabbed his hanky on the afflicted area. As though an earthquake split the Earth's face and lava spewed forth from the passageway, the cardinal red liquid of life feverishly gushed through the open wounds soaking then staining the cotton overlay. Philip's life was frantically bleeding away one hanky at a time. The dye was cast. He prayed.

By morning, with prayers unfulfilled, Philip's anxiety escalated as did the infection that brewed overnight. With lips pus-filled and swollen shut, the intense pain surrounding Philip's mouth were no match for the agony yet to come. Helen took immediate action as she always did, and before he could count the notes on the scale, he and Helen were on the trolley headed to the office of the nearest doctor whose expertise, by all accounts, spanned the gamut from curing the common cold and the chicken pox to delivering newborns and prescribing vitamins. But Philip's situation did not fall into the category of norm. His was a unique medical circumstance requiring that which was nonexistent - a specialist.

What does a family doctor know about the delicacy of trumpeter's lips? Now what? Philip lamented.

With no options available and swelling at the acute level, trust had to be given to the medic at hand. After careful observation and evaluation, the doctor delivered the fatal blow in the form of one word – surgery.

Upon completion of the procedure, Philip awoke to his worst nightmare. He assessed the result that would forever define his musical life. With his tongue, he swiped the area and surveyed what was left of his lip. ***My God! What has he done? What have I done?***

Philip agonized at the debilitating realization that his upper lip – his trumpet playing lip – was gone. In that instant of excruciating mental torture, the same knife blade that slashed and ripped apart his lip plunged deep into his chest and ruptured his heart. Suffocating under the deluge of tears, Philip's essence collapsed; his dreams shattered and torn to shreds by misplaced incisions; his musical life in ruins.

"I played like there was no tomorrow" he sobbed to me often when I was a kid. "I thought I'd be able to play forever."

His dreams pulverized, he smothered to the point of lifelessness beneath the crushing tonnage of the universe that had collapsed in on him.

"I knew I'd never play again."

After surgery, Philip's trumpet lip was dead. Suture scars and the permanence of disfigurement, like a reoccurring, horrific nightmare, tortured him with an overwhelming sense of loss every minute of every day for the remainder of his life. Grief stricken and in mourning at his own death, Philip bypassed purgatory and went straight to hell.

Relating this story to me never failed to make both of us cry. As his daughter and a horn player myself, I understood and empathized better than anyone else, and even though I was only a child and years removed from his frightening, life-altering tragedy, I felt his agonizing pain as though it was my own. We cried together.

"I wish I had your lip," he moaned.

"I wish I could give it to you, Yurtz," I sighed.

And although this conversation repeated itself too many times to calculate, we cried with each reiteration. I would have given up my life had I been able to give him my lip.

Most of humanity at that time would have viewed a man weeping as a sign of weakness to be ridiculed. Not me. Not the musicians who witnessed his torment. As I saw it, Yurtz's propensity towards emotional displays were signs of courage and of strength, as it took those qualities to do that which society deemed emasculating. Even while watching the news on the television, there were a great many outbursts of tears for those whom Yurtz did not even know but whose lives had been stricken with tragedy. He felt their pain as his own, and I admired him greatly for his sensitivity and compassion towards humankind. My deepest prayer was that his own pain would somehow, sometime, someday be relieved. But that never happened in his lifetime.

For the first time in his life, Philip sought help from a trumpet instructor who, baffled by Philip's predicament, was at a loss to offer any viable solutions. Taking matters into his own hands, Philip's resolve took control of his own situation. "I had to do something. I had to get my lip back. I just had to get my lip back!"

Without an upper lip, playing the trumpet became a challenge of daunting enormity. Philip attempted to blow from the side of his mouth; then blow with his bottom lip doubled over into the mouthpiece. At one point he grew a mustache to add bulk to a lip that was not there. Switching mouthpieces became a daily necessity in an attempt to find one that might allow him to play. There were mouthpieces with varying circumferences, thicknesses, size openings, and shaft lengths. From the Couesnon Paris mouthpiece to the Parduba Double Cup #5 to the Holton Heim #2 to the Bach #'s 6, 6C, 5B, 1 ¼ C, 10 C. He kept those among the many tested.

When questioned why he just simply did not change his instrument, he lamented, "I love the trumpet so much that I'm gonna play even if it hurts."

After countless hours of trial and error lip positioning and mouthpiece selection, he regained **some** of his embrasure.

Road roommate Saul assessed Philip's end result. "With a dead arm and only half a lip, still no one played better!"

Yurtz would have been humbled by that remark only recently made, but he still would not have been satisfied with what he could produce on his horn. He forever anguished that he had lost the ability "to play what I'm thinking. My head is way ahead of my lip. I can fool anyone but myself."

And for that, he could not be consoled.

8

The Band Meets Society

Late 1930's – Early 1940's

Philip would never fully recover from his traumatic surgery, yet he recovered sufficiently enough to return to the Troubadours. Saul was amazed that he "was the only guy I ever saw that played the horn from the side of his mouth!"

Although the boys were still teenagers, the music of the Vernon Troubadours had outgrown the teen style. It was time for a change. Touting themselves as a Society Band, the group selected their handsome pianist, Joel Palmer, as the front man and new leader. The **Joel Palmer Orchestra** took birth.

With the evolution of a new identity and image, the young dappers donned three variations of tuxedoes; the slickest, most eye-catching one featured double-breasted cream colored jackets enhanced by chocolate brown slacks. To complete the look, they selected matching chocolate brown bow ties and chocolate brown lapel flowers.

The group was as extraordinary musically as the combination of tuxedo colors. All of the guys grew up together within blocks of each other and attended Hamilton Elementary and Nichols Junior High Schools. "We were like family – all brothers."

The rebirth of the group began at the Red Cup, a dance hall and club where Cross County Center in Yonkers, New York now sits. They rocked the house five nights a week and, according to Saul, musicians from all over Westchester County and Manhattan would frequent the club to listen to the band swing.

In the early 1930's their popularity soared. For three years the band jammed at the Lawrence Inn in Mamaroneck, New York six nights a week and on Sunday afternoons from two to four. At that same venue the orchestra broadcast live on radio station WFAS three times a week. The radio station was flooded with requests. Word travels, and the Joel Palmer Orchestra was about to do the same.

With notice from their booking agent, the boys hit the road and landed for the first time in Richmond, Virginia. Phil immediately fell in love with the city and the surrounding area. At the time, there were few hotels or hotel chains. Local residents housed members of traveling entertainers.

"The residents loved us," Saul related proudly. "For all the years we traveled, there were never any arguments. No one in our group ever got drunk, took drugs, or got into trouble. We were all good guys."

Each member of the Palmer crew paid seven dollars for their weekly room and board in a row house on Grace Street in Richmond. The awkward rooming situation made strange bedfellows. Although there were several beds in a room, the lack of space necessitated that two guys share each bed. "It's just the way it was on the road." But not much time was spent in those tight quarters as gigs went late into the evenings infringing on the early morning. Philip and Saul were bedmates, and they developed a brother bond that lasted for the rest of their lives.

The room was invariably second to the board. For seven dollars weekly, the guys received lavish, homemade breakfasts and dinners that typified southern hospitality. To sweeten the deal further, upon the completion of their evening entertainment and their arrival home at two or three in the morning, the boys were treated to coffee, cake, and light fare to hold them over until the big breakfast the next morning. Savoring every bite and practically licking his plate clean at every sitting, Philly was a compliment to every chef. He could not wait for the next meal, and everyone knew it.

Joel Palmer recalled the story that occurred in Lynchburg, Virginia in 1941. The guys were accommodated on the second floor of a private home owned by Mrs. Rogers. When she announced mealtime by ringing a bell, the guys jumped up and raced down the stairs, Philly invariably leading the charge. It was well documented that because of Phil's perfect pitch, he could not hear high pitched sounds such as birds chirping or bells ringing. Thus the ploy was set.

It was late afternoon, hardly late enough for dinner. The guys suddenly jumped up and ran towards the stairs as though they had heard the dinner bell. Taking their cue, Philly took a flying leap bounding over everyone, who let him pass with ease. He raced down the staircase and plopped himself at the table. Having thought she had heard a noise, Mrs. Rogers, who knew each fellow by name, peeked into the dining room and spotted Philly at his seat. "Phil?" she wondered. Philly's eyes lit up in anticipation of the forthcoming goodies. "What are you doing here at this time? Dinner is not for another hour and a half!"

Phil made his way back up to the second floor where he was greeted by nine laughing hyenas. "We had a good laugh," Joel wrote, but "nobody ever laughed harder than Philly" even if he was the brunt of the joke.

Philip may have been the brunt of many a dinner joke, but no one ever joked when it concerned his perfect pitch. That was one sacred area the man was always right. One could bet a life's savings on it, not to mention betting life itself on it.

Each evening before the start of one of their sets, Joel Palmer would ask Phil to come to the microphone. "I'm sure all you music fans know the meaning of perfect pitch," Joel acknowledged. "One of the members of our band, trumpet fellow Phil Keen, has it. We will now test his ability and ask him to name the chord I play."

Joel played a different chord on the piano each evening then motioned to Phil who promptly responded with the name of the chord. "Now name the individual notes in that chord." Dependent upon the particular chord that had been played, Phil revealed the notes: "C – E – G – B Flat!"

"With that amazing demonstration and the crowd cheering," Joel explained, "I would have Phil take the three-note pick up to Stardust followed by the orchestra accompaniment. This was always a highlight of the evening."

Upon hearing of the highlight of every evening, an old hometown friend from the West Side was intrigued. "Tell me, Phil. After a solo did you ever get a standing ovation?"

Phil's response was immediate. "Yeah, man. Many times!"

Obviously impressed and genuinely wanting to hear all the details, the buddy exclaimed then questioned further. "Wow! That's great. What song were you playing?"

Without skipping a beat, Phil retorted, "The Star Spangled Banner!"

Always the jokester even when it involved his playing, it was difficult to get a straight answer no matter the question. Phil's buddy shook his head realizing he should have known better than to try to get the scoop from a clown. The two men howled as they made their way down the street.

The band enjoyed months booked as the house band at the Tantilla Gardens on Broad Street in Richmond, Virginia, across from where the Holiday Inn stands today. On the Tantilla Gardens stage, a massive Joel Palmer Orchestra marquee hung on the iridescent silver backdrop curtain and attested to the group's collective dream becoming reality at last.

"Another group of guys probably would not have stayed together for the little money we made. But we were brothers and in it for the long haul." Earning thirty dollars for a six to seven gig week, the orchestra played dance and stage music composed and arranged by Phil, his innate genius at work since the group's inception and for its duration.

Joel Palmer recalled that Phil "made great arrangements, especially the one of Swanee River with Hank taking the lead on baritone sax accompanied by the other sax men. He was part of our three vocal groups and his harmony was out of this world." In a letter dated in 2001, Joel indicated that he and Phil collaborated on "a lovely song called The Stars Up Above (Will Bring Us Together When We Are Apart), and although the written music has been "lost somewhere", it remains a favorite. Joel proudly scribed that his granddaughter, then eleven years old, loves to play jazz piano. "Would you believe, I showed her some 'hot licks' that Phil used in some of our arrangements and she loves to play them!"

As Saul recalled, "Phil was the band. If it wasn't for him, there would have been no band. He wrote every chart we ever played and was really our true leader. He wrote every piece of music and led every rehearsal. And with his perfect pitch, we could never have been out of tune. He wouldn't have it any other way but in perfect tune at all times. As part of our vocal trio, 'The Three Cheers', his vocal harmony was out of this world. And the way he used the electric guitar in arrangements was unique for the times."

As Saul continued to reminisce, the sparkle and joy of his remembrances radiated so brightly that the Sun itself would have been blinded. "Phil even created novelty bits. An audience favorite was the bit where each guy took out a toy piano that was hidden behind his stand. We stood in a row on the bandstand and played the tunes Phil had worked out for us. There we were ten guys playing Tippy, Tippy, Tippy Tim in harmony on toy pianos – another Phil original. He was a one of a kind in every way!"

Richmond and The Tantilla Gardens became home base for the Palmer band. After several weeks at the Gardens, the band traveled to various club dates where their booking agent had secured dates. In 1940 the guys headed back north to Flushing Meadows, New York to perform in the 1939 World's Fair Aquacade, a special amphitheater seating upwards of 10,000 people. From this venue the orchestra broadcast live, and a tape recording of one of their radio broadcast sessions is part of my memorabilia.

December of 1941. The tour continued with full speed ahead, and the popular swing ensemble was on the move from one venue to another: north to the Crooked Lake Hotel in Saratoga, New York – back to the Tantilla Gardens in Richmond – out to Rehoboth Beach Country Club in Delaware for a steady four weeks – back to Virginia's Tantilla Gardens – north to Massachusetts – south to Virginia. Everywhere they performed, the audiences were jumping.

"They loved us in Lynchburg!" Saul bragged with fondness. In addition to performing two theater shows daily, every military school and university in the area between and around Virginia's towns of Lynchburg and Christiansburg was set afire with the hot sounds of the big band. All through the tour, the band enjoyed the crowds who thrived on their originality and sizzling style.

Near Worchester, Massachusetts, the boys lived in the house next to the club where they were booked. During the day, Angelo, the sax man, became Angelo, the short-order cook at a local greasy spoon. The boys devoured Angelo's oily concoctions, as no one in the group was a gourmand requiring fancy creations. The food was good, but the value even better. No matter the fare or the quantity consumed, Angelo charged each one of the band members a whopping fifteen cents per meal. With consumption on the conspicuous rise but the cash flow in the register in stagnation, the owner's suspicion kicked in. After two weeks of the same eight member crew gorging themselves voraciously, he finally realized that the pack was gnawing at his daily profits – sixteen eggs, sixteen strips of bacon, sixteen slices of toast, eight baloney sandwiches, eight tuna fish sandwiches, sixteen grill cheese sandwiches, and thirty-two cups of coffee at a time. Angelo's days as chief cook and register attendant were over. Luckily, the guys were pretty full by then!

The road trips were tough. Along with the month-long stays, there were many one-nighters with miles between to travel to the next destination. Countless thousands of miles were trekked from one venue to another. The entourage consisted of men in two cars and one van carrying both the instruments and several band members, including Philip. On one jaunt from Richmond, Virginia to Raleigh, South Carolina, the three vehicles were slated to meet at the site of the club date. "A few guys got to the place – the others never showed up", Yurtz recalled. The van carrying the instruments and one car met as scheduled. Those that were on site waited until time ran out. The group was expected to play, and they had no choice but to do so. Worried yet under contract, the mini-band wailed as though nothing was wrong. The audience, unaware that part of the band was missing, had a ball as they danced through the sets. Upon the completion of the evening, word arrived that the other musicians had been in a horrific accident, landing those in that car in the hospital. Bass player, Joe Tanno, most seriously injured and lucky to be alive, spent months in the hospital recuperating.

Because road life was draining, the guys took turns taking short trips home to Mount Vernon for some needed rest. As faith would have it, Phil's break would turn out to be his lucky one.

9

Something About Mary

The timing could not have been better. Phil was home enjoying a respite from the madness of road life. But just as he was settling in for the night, a knock at the door disturbed his serenity.

"Hey, Philly! I haven't seen you in months!"

The two Italian men hugged.

"Yeah, man. I've been on the road. Got home yesterday for a few days rest."

"Well, you're in luck. There's a small party at Josephine's tonight, and we're going!"

"Listen, Gino. I'd love to go, but I'm tired," Phil reminded his buddy of his intention to relax.

Not one to take no for an answer, Gino kept prodding. "What'a ya gonna do home alone? Come on, man. It'll be a good time with old friends."

The pleading continued to the point of wearing Phil into submission. "O.K. But just for a little while."

Upon arrival, Phil scanned the room and focused on the one person in the intimate group of six that he had not known. Introductions made, Phil found Mary of particular interest. Both parties reticent and awkward hardly said a word to each other. Still, there seemed to be something intriguing about each for the other.

Having been mesmerized by Mary's natural beauty – a cascading, massive mane framing a perfectly shaped oval face, a pure olive complexion, skin as luxuriously smooth as silk, a beauty mark on the upper left lip enhanced by a cosmetic pencil, and deep brown eyes encircled by a green halo – he really had not noticed the rest of the five foot two inch package.

A glance here – a smile there, and all too soon it was time to leave. The group left in tandem and attempted to squeeze into the only car available. Whether by chance or design, Mary found herself on Philly's lap! Not that she minded, but Philly had some difficulty supporting Mary's two hundred thirty pound frame!

Not that it mattered. He was going on the road in a few days anyway.

10

Revelations

The road proved hectic and lonely. For reasons unbeknownst to Philly, he could not get Mary out of his mind. He liked her as a friend, "only a friend", and yet, he felt the inexplicable urge to send her cards and notes from the road.

The alluring, legendary club names enticed customers and charmed Mary. From her station in life, Mary's realm was, at best, suited for romanticizing about the societal upper-crust who, unlike herself, had the wherewithal to frequent the likes of The Gingham Gardens, The Rainbow Room, The Terraced Gardens, The Skyway Ballroom, The Lake Club, The Blue Moon, The Palm Beach Café, The Grand, The Westwood Supper Club, and The Palace. Descriptive addendums furthered their appeal and Mary's imagery and fancies. The Beverly Hills Country Club in Newport, Kentucky, touted as "The Show Place of the Middle West", and The Tantilla Gardens of Richmond, Virginia, highly revered as "The South's Most Beautiful Ballroom" were most notable in conjuring up her fantasies. Mary was thoroughly enamored by the glamour of the far-off places around the country that she could only dream of. Leave Mount Vernon? Never happen in her lifetime.

Taking another break from the tour, Philly and Mary met by chance on Fourth Avenue where Mary worked at a small ice cream parlor. The two agreed to a cup of coffee at the Beehive, a small hometown eatery perfect for small talk. They walked passed the lengthy luncheonette counter eyeing the pastry choices and assorted breads and muffins that remained fresh beneath the glass dome cake dishes. Although the counter stools were comfortable, they were not conducive to chatting face to face. The couple opted for one of the cozier booths in the rear of the restaurant.

Somewhat more at ease in the art of conversation, Mary made her first disclosure. "I was born on December 24th and given the Italian name for baby – Bambina – in honor of the Baby Jesus. Bambina is the actual name on my birth certificate."

"So, how'd you become Mary?" Phil queried.

"Well," Mary explained, "when I was christened, the church officials refused to accept a non-sanctioned Catholic name. So, I was renamed Mary in honor of the closest person to Baby Jesus – his mother, Mary."

Phil joked about the incident in elementary school that instigated his own name change from Felice to Phil.

As they conversed, their commonalities became evident. Both were products of Italian immigrants. Mary's parents both hailed from the town of Acri in the Cosenza region of the southern providence of Calabria. Her mom, Santa Groccia, was from a rather wealthy family as she traveled first class to America where she met and married the not so wealthy Angelo Curto.

Philip's parents were from the Campobasso region of central Italy, though not from the same town. Felice Lucchini, born in the town of Peligna, and Marianne Petti, born in the town of Casalciprano, met and married in Italy before traveling with several children to America.

Both Mary and Phil came from large families who suffered with the loss of children as infants. In Mary's family at least two children did not live past infancy while at least two and possibly as many as four infants did not survive in Phil's family. Even in the land of opportunity, life was constant struggle for both families – survival a hardship for all concerned.

Both families lost their homes. Mary's house burned to the ground. Having lost everything, the Red Cross provided assistance until the family could get back on its feet and relocate as renters at 225 South

Ninth Avenue. Philip's parents lost their house at 18 South Bond Street when their small grocery store on Mount Vernon Avenue went into bankruptcy during the Depression. They relocated as renters at 10 South Bond Street.

"On a lighter note," Phil sparked with pride, "my Pop is a music maker!"

"And my Papa is a wine maker!" Mary quipped. "He has two barrels in the cellar behind the house. It's always cold under ground beneath the garage so the temperature is naturally controlled. The problem is that it is so dark down there no one can see what he actually puts in his vats. Sometimes we wonder if *he* can see what he's putting in! But I guess its okay. Everyone who drinks his wine is still alive!" Laughing while sipping from their second cup of coffee, Mary warned, "But don't expect a free sample. Even his best friends over for a visit are charged for each sour tasting, vinegary drink!"

The flow of words hastened as their comfort zone widened.

"I almost died as a baby," Phil revealed. "I was having problems breathing, and my body was actually blue from lack of oxygen. Do you believe it? I was put on the warm oven door while my parents prayed to Saint Joseph. Some beginning to life! Well, I'm here today, so I guess I had a guardian angel watching over me."

Mary shivered as she recounted her childhood experience. "When I was a little girl, an angel – I'm sure it was my sister Louise who died at the age of one – came to me at the foot of my bed. *Come with me Mary. I'll take you home.* No! I told her. I was afraid to go with her. *It is a beautiful place.* No! *Please come with me to this beautiful place where we can play together.* No! I kept saying, no! The angel image left me, and I woke up in a sweat!"

"That's eerie! She must have been frightening!" Philly assumed.

"Oh, no! I wasn't afraid of the angel– just of dying and leaving my family."

"Has she ever returned to you?" Phil fretted.

"No, but I think of her all the time. I'm sure she's watching over me keeping me safe."

It was agreed that guardian angels no matter the form were comforting. The waitress returned with the third fill of each cup, and the intrigue of discovering more about each other continued.

It was revealed that both had attended Edison Technical and Vocational High School. Neither having graduated, both parties cited incidences involved in their decisions to leave school prematurely.

Minding her business and quietly walking to her next tenth grade class, Mary was spotted then singled out by the principal. "Young lady!" the principal pointed at Mary and motioned for her to stand opposite him.

"Yes, sir", Mary replied as she had been taught the respectful and proper way to address those older than she.

"What is **that** on your face?" he inquired as he leaned towards Mary giving her a look that frightened her.

Mary grabbed her face; her hand searching for the abnormality he was staring at. But not feeling any maladies or inconsistencies there, she questioned, "On my face?"

"Don't get smart with me, young lady! What is that dark, red paint?"

"Oh!" Mary smiled then blushed as she held her hands up to her mouth. "It's lipstick!" she explained not realizing her grave mistake.

"Well, apparently, there are no rules in your house, but in my house – this school – there are rules. And you, my dear, are breaking one of them."

"What rule?" Mary whimpered wondering what she had done so wrong to capture the attention and ire of the principal.

"Lipstick is not allowed in school, missy," he advised with a warning attached. "You get that paint off your lips right now, and I had better never see you wearing it again!"

Although Mary thought the inquisition was over, she was wrong. Without provocation on her part, she suddenly felt a painful blow as the back of the principal's hand slapped her right across her face!

Sobbing, Mary left the building immediately and ran home to safety – or so she thought.

Mary raced into the house and headed for the kitchen where she was certain she would be cradled in the arms of her loving, gentle mother. Not a chance in Mary's world. There was only one person in the kitchen at that moment – her father, a no-nonsense man whose strict disciplinary inclinations were not to be tested even under the best of circumstances. Seated at the kitchen table, he glared at the clock and then at Mary. "Why are you home so early from school?" he inquired with his usual gruff voice. "And what are you crying about?"

Through the tears and the sniffling, Mary attempted to explain as best she could. "The principal slapped me for wearing lipstick in school. He said lipstick was not allowed there, but I didn't know that. Then he slapped my face!"

"Well, if the principal said lipstick is not allowed, then it is not allowed. A rule is a rule."

Mary could not believe that her father, stern as he was yet still her protector, was siding with the principal.

"And you, my dear Mary," he continued as he rose from his chair, "will not wear lipstick in this house either!"

With that assertion and to further his command of the situation, Mary's father hauled off with the back of his hand slapping her even harder than the principal did. Mary never returned to school. She opted for a job. At least at work she could help the family financially and not get beaten up for it.

Phil was in the last semester of the eleventh grade when his school days ended. A month-long class project was underway in the shop. A group of guys were fooling around pushing and shoving each other when one of the guys accidentally plowed into the table where the project rested. The table crashed into the wall sending the project aloft before it tumbled to the floor, splattering into tiny pieces. Philly, the usual jokester of the group, was on the complete opposite side of the room at the time, but the shop teacher immediately blamed him for the catastrophe. Philip vehemently denied the accusations. With everyone in the class knowing the true culprits yet no one willing to confess, Philip took the hit.

"Pick up every last piece," the teacher ordered. "You will stay after school for the rest of your life, if necessary, to put this project back together."

"But, sir," Phil protested. "I didn't do it!"

"Everyone here, including me, knows it was you."

Philip was deeply disappointed and hurt that the guilty parties would not fess up to their actions, but he would never rat out the real perpetrators. With no one stepping forward to claim responsibility,

Phil pleaded his own case. "How could I have knocked over the project when I was on the other side of the room and no where near it?"

"Pick up those pieces now!" the teacher growled while the rest of the group stood there letting Philip be the fall-guy.

Philip could have picked up the pieces, but why should he? He was not to blame.

"I did not do it," Phil defended once again, "and I will not pick up those pieces!"

"Boy!" the teacher challenged with open anger and contempt for Philip. "Don't argue with me, boy. **Pick up those pieces or get out!**"

The ultimatum given, Philip walked out and never returned.

Phil knew who did it. All the guys knew but kept their mouths shut. It bothered him the rest of his life as he retold that story many times. I even know who did it, but will not declare that which has been kept under wraps for so long. Besides, the deed was done too long ago to make a difference now. For Philip, the true realization of the consequences of his decision did not occur to him in that moment of anger and frustration. Not until adulthood would that incident cost him dearly.

Not having picked up those shop project pieces translated into not picking up the most important piece of all – a piece of paper affirming a high school education. But what did a diploma mean to a teen about to blossom in his true field of endeavor. He was a gifted musician set in his career choice, and that was all that mattered at that time.

Sitting in the booth at the coffee shop, Phil and Mary continued to divulge their lives to one another one incident at a time. A few revelations later, they parted ways with Philip off to musically conquer the world.

11

It's A Losing Proposition

Early 1940's

With Philly back on the road, Mary continued her hum-drum life now with a sense of purpose. Philly had no idea of what was to come.

"I'm going home for a few days," announced Phil's road roommate Saul. "This traveling is getting to me, and I need a short break. Is there anything I can do for you while I'm home?"

Philly's eyes lit up. "Well, yeah. Maybe you can look up my friend Mary, and say hello to her for me."

"Where can I find her?" Saul questioned.

"She works at the ice cream parlor next to the Beehive on Fourth Avenue. Do you know where I mean?" Of course, Saul knew the place, but Philly just needed to be reassured.

"Yeah, I know the place. But how will I know Mary?"

Phil could not help smiling. "Man – you can't miss her!"

"What'a ya talking about, Phil? Ya gotta describe her for me," Saul demanded.

"She's beautiful!"

"Mount Vernon's loaded with beautiful dames. Ya gotta describe her better than that," Saul insisted.

"Well, Saul, she's the most beautiful two hundred-thirty pound girl in the place."

"Wait a minute. Are you telling me your girl is two hundred-thirty pounds for real?"

"Yeah", Phil sighed, "but she is beautiful."

Saul took off still thinking Phil had been on the road a little too long. Nonetheless, he promised he would look for Mary, and he would never disappoint his best buddy. When he entered the ice cream parlor, Saul quickly eyed a lovely woman standing at the counter.

"Hi! My name is Saul." He cordially introduced himself then stated his purpose. "I'm here looking for Mary."

"I'm Mary!"

The response from this beauty was totally unexpected. Saul squinted then gazed again at the vision before him. *No*, he contemplated. *This slender, hourglass figured girl can not possibly be the Mary I am looking for.*

"Oh", he said qualifying himself. "I'm looking for the **other** Mary."

"Well, I'm the **only** Mary here!"

Saul took another gander at the beauty now smiling at him and figured he had been duped. *Leave it to Philly to play a joke sending me on a wild goose chase to find some dame that does not exist. A two hundred-thirty pounder? I'll get him for this!*

Saul was a bit miffed not only at his chum for the ploy that put him into this awkward position, but more so at himself, the chump for believing there might have been such a girl.

Since the gag certainly was not the fault of the looker in front of him, Saul could not nor would not take the prank out on her. The gentleman offered his sincerest apology. "Sorry to have bothered you, miss."

She returned the gesture of a lady with the have a nice day smile.

Saul stepped towards the door muttering under his breath, "When I get that Philly, I'm gonna.........."

"Philly?" the young doll gasped. "Did I hear you say Philly?" Mary's heart fluttered faster than a hummingbird's.

"Oh. You do know Phil Keen?" Saul took a huge gulp of air. "Are you by any chance Philly's Mary?"

"Yes, I guess that's me!" Mary could hardly contain her excitement in the prospect that she was Philly's Mary.

Stymied and confused by the cover girl model that stood before him, Saul gasped. "So, you're Mary? You're Phil's Mary?"

With a smile wider than the length of Mount Vernon, Mary reaffirmed, "That's right. I'm Phil's Mary!"

"So – you're Mary." Totally baffled, Saul's perplexed facial expression telegraphed his confusion. "So – if you're Mary – where's your other half?"

Giggling, Mary blushed into a rose petal hue. Yes, she was Philly's Mary – the same Mary – only one hundred pounds less of her! All those months of determination – of sacrifice – of starvation – of unimaginable will-power – of denying herself the pleasures of the Italian cuisine she dearly loved – all of this was finally paying off in a big way.

Saul was busting a gut to tell Phil, but how would he do it?

12

Hold That Tiger

Saul could not wait to get back on the road – or rather get back at Phil.

"How's good old Mount Vernon?" Phil tried to seem interested with his trite question. It was not about the town but about a certain person that he really wanted to ask about.

"It's still there." Saul affirmed.

"Hey, that's my line." Phil paused to gather his nerve. "Uh, did you find Mary?"

"Yeah."

"Well? Did you tell her I said hello?"

"Yeah."

"So, what'd she say?"

"Hello to you too!" Saul nodded his head nonchalantly as though that had been the extent of the entire conversation.

This stalling tactic was finally getting the normally mellow Phil riled. "Come on, man. Is that it?. So what else did she say? And how is she?"

"Well, it happened since you've been gone," Saul informed.

"What'a ya mean it happened? Is she okay? What's wrong?"

"I gotta tell ya, Phil. Your girl is only half there."

"Half there?" Phil, the usual jester now anguished as he repeated, "Half there? You mean – she's gone crazy?"

The frightened look on Philly's face gave Saul the realization that enough was enough and that this little ploy was no longer funny. *Can't joke with a man in love* he figured. Saul knew it was time to give it to Phil straight. "No. She's not crazy!"

Confused, Phil growled, "So what's this 'half there' bit?"

"Well, since you've been on the road, my man, Mary has lost one hundred pounds!"

Philip could not fathom what he had heard. "A hundred pounds?"

"That's what I said," Saul repeated, "one hundred pounds. Only half of your girl is left – and what a half that is! I guess she's crazy about you, and you will be the crazy one if you don't grab a hold of her right away.!"

13

A Proposal?

Phil could hardly wait to see his girl. Whatever half was left, he knew it was the best half a guy could hope for.

Years later, both concurred that they "never really had a date. We walked everywhere holding hands with Uncle Tommy Castelli as chaperone. He never left us alone!" Still, they managed to have their first kiss in Gino's convertible rumble seat. It was divine, but would it come to an end?

Once again Phil and Mary met at the Beehive. Mary was nervous about the inevitable about to take place. She knew it was time for Philly to join the band but had no inkling as to what was to be offered. Neither did Philly for that matter.

Phil looked unusually downtrodden. "Mary. I have to re-join the guys. I'll be away for a few months – maybe four or five. I'm not sure right now how long this road trip will last."

In the face of yet another separation, Mary remained relatively composed. She had known for days that this conversation was going to take place. And she certainly did not want to put Philly under any more pressure than he was already compressed under. Phil appreciated Mary's understanding nature, and he admired her for it. His departure would be less stressful knowing Mary would be there when he returned.

But *how long will she be there? How long was she willing to wait?* Phil mulled over these thoughts for weeks. Saul had told him to get his act together or he might lose the love of his life.

"I'll write," Mary promised.

"Me, too," Phil promised likewise.

A lull came over the couple. They sat looking down at the table as there was not much else to be said. Separation had happened so often – too often. Was it time for a change? Their relationship threatened, Phil had to do something. Before he could catch his words, his voice broke the silence.

"Next time I come home – maybe, we'll get married then."

Did he just propose? Mary was uncertain, but willing to take the chance that he had done just that.

"Yes!" Mary blurted out before he could change his mind. "Yes!"

14

It Was All In The Cards

1943

The date was set – February 7, 1943. It would be in the dead of winter, but the tour necessitated the choice. Certainly summer or fall would have been preferred, but for Mary, the time was right no matter the month selected.

While Philly was away playing, Mary was home planning. All but one colossal detail fell into place – the gown. Size would have presented an immense problem had Mary still tipped the scale at two hundred-thirty pounds. A part of Mary was missing with the loss of that dreaded one hundred pounds, but the part of her that would dream big, would never be lost. It was her turn to fantasize as every young woman her age. She envisioned herself in stately grandeur, her hourglass figure delicately draped in a lavish Cinderella ball gown being whisked away by her prince. As she and her prince whirled clutched in each other's grasp, the music in her heart faded into silence. Stark reality hit hard. There would be no ball gown. For this princess, the purchase of a gown, even for the most important occasion of her life, was monetarily out of the question. Barring the lipstick incident, with Mary's family destitute, she really did have to quit school before the completion of the tenth grade so she could earn money for staples.

At Christmas, Mary and her four siblings each received an apple or a pear and a hand full of nuts, and although it seemed that Santa missed their house, all were grateful for the little that he left. Because it was Mary's birthday, she received a little something extra in her stocking – a nickel. How could she ever afford a gown? What could she possibly wear that would not disappoint the love of her life waiting for her at the end of the isle? She needed Cinderella's very own fairy Godmother to intervene in this crisis.

The fairy Godmother appeared as Helen, the sister who saved Philip's life as an infant. Working her magic, Helen now saved Mary. A master at the sewing machine, Helen designed then created a wedding ensemble befitting royalty, and, on her special day, Mary would be that princess she so often dreamt of.

Family and friends gathered at Our Lady of Mount Carmel Church on First Street. Philly waited anxiously at the foot of the white marble altar, his best man, Tommy, by his side. He had never been this nervous, not even when playing in front of hundreds or even thousands. Thank goodness the organ bellowed so as to drown out Philly's percussive heart.

The bride appeared in the vestibule. A collective congregational gasp nearly sucked in the rafters. Mary's angelic aura stunned the gathered. More regal than even Philly could have envisioned; his eyes would have popped loose had they not been affixed to their sockets. As Mary stood on the white satin runner gathering the strength to walk into a new chapter of her life, all eyes fixated on her majesty.

With emphasis on elegance and sophistication, the silk brocade, intricately embossed, long sleeve gown graced Mary's frame. Attention to meticulous detail evident, hundreds of cloth-covered buttons embellished the outline of the front of the gown lining the modified v-shape down towards the waist. One row of buttons placed horizontally just below the shoulder line on either side enhanced the beauty of the design. The entire back of the dress from the neck to the floor was garnished with the same appliquéd buttons. Attached to the back of the straight-line bodice flowed a lengthy train, which lagged behind on the white runner then wrapped around the front for photographs.

A veil from the mid-section of her hair gently fell to the back of her knees. Mary's voluptuous mane, pulled back over her ears, flowed down her back behind the veil. With only one refinement to her face being the deep red lipstick that she was once slapped for wearing, a pompadour style coiffure allowed full view of the splendor of her radiant face. The simple adornment of a heart-shaped pendant hung perfectly in the v of the gown and served as a reminder of the love she was about to share. Mary's favorite flower, the daisy, completed her ensemble. The massive bouquet of aromatic flowers spanned the length from her bust-line to below mid-thigh and covered the width of her hips. Possibly one of the largest bouquets ever to be carried down the isle by a non-royal, the Highness would not be outdone on her special day.

Vows taken, the guests headed to the reception on South Ninth Avenue where they gathered for what was hardly a white-glove affair. Though commencing in the basement of the Curto's rental residence, the well-wishers were treated royally. Even the colorful backdrop decoration had its own unique flavor. Hundreds of jars of Mamma Curto's homemade tomato sauce, whole tomatoes, peaches, and pears made from Grandpa Curto's backyard garden lined the concrete basement walls from ceiling to floor. Philly's mouth watered for the second time in the past hour and a half. First there was Mary, and now the tomatoes. Or was Mary the tomato? Anyway, he did love them both, and savored the anticipation of his feasts. Location aside, the hearty Italian banquet therein was fit for this gent and his lady.

Amid the festivities a bit of business required immediate attention. The transaction involved those most prized envelopes and the cards within that held the wherewithal to begin a life's journey for two. And, as much of their life to come, Philip and Mary's cards held a royal flush of sorts. Before scampering off to catch the next train, the bride and groom had to deduct the first $35 from their gifts to pay for the use of the basement!

The newlyweds scurried off to their destiny with $18 between them. From the cellar on South Ninth Avenue to the cellar of New York's Grand Central Station, there was no time to waste and no honeymoon to garner. The guys in the band would be awaiting their arrival in Richmond, Virginia. The show must go on.

15

On The Road Again And For The First Time

Mary could not believe she was somewhere other than Mount Vernon. *Virginia. A beautiful name for a beautiful State*, she thought. Philly said it was, and although she was yet to emerge from the train station, she was in total agreement completely captivated by her new surroundings. *So charming. So elegant. So dainty. So, where are the ladies in their gowns and parasols? Oh, that must be South Carolina.* Mary's thoughts wandered through a myriad of fairy tale images.

"Come on, Babe!" Phil summoned. Mary's serenity was jolted back to reality. "Saul is waiting to take us to the house. We have to get ready for tonight's performance at the Tantilla Gardens."

With a trumpet case and one, half-empty suitcase, the car was loaded within a minute, which was not fast enough for Mary. She could not contain her excitement not even for a nanosecond. As the car revved up, Mary raced in overdrive, her anticipatory palpitations quite evident to her new husband seated next to her and holding her hand. As foreign and as distant as the landscape on another continent, the new vista encircled Mary with an awe inspiring scenery that seemed to float past her window as do the clouds that float past angels in heaven. And, at that moment in time, Mary was in heaven. She was, after all, in

Richmond, Virginia, the closest place to heaven on Earth for one who had never left the four square mile city of Mount Vernon, New York.

If Philly was over anxious to get to a favorite destination, Mary was even more impatient nearly leaping out of her skin in anticipation of her arrival there. For Mary, just the mere mention of the Tantilla Gardens was enough to land her in Eden. There was no question as to why it was one of Philly's favorite nightclubs. The grand ballroom at The Tantilla Gardens was large enough for eighteen hundred hoofers who could dance, as music librarian Liz Underwood described, "cheek to cheek without bumping bumpers." Mary was eager to be one of those eighteen hundred breathless dancers swinging and swaying to the beat of the Joel Palmer Orchestra.

With their two-week stint over, the band moved to their next destination. There were times on the road when life was like being on a giant non-stop amusement park ride, especially when it involved night gigs in one town and late night transport to a different town for the next evening's show. And for Mary, this roller coaster was no free ride. To supplement the less than minimum wage the musicians earned, Mary waited tables in every town by day. Evenings found Mary on the dance floor shuffling her way through the nighttime sets. It was exhausting, but she admitted to having the time of her life.

Mary loved meeting new people, and they loved her. Her limitless energy and enthusiasm coupled with her radiant warmth was the magnet that drew others to her. In fact, after the touring days ended, Mary required a head start – as early as September – when writing upwards of three hundred fifty Christmas and Hanukkah cards. In turn, we received as many from all over the country.

And Mary's correspondences did not end there. Birthday, anniversary, get well, thank you, thinking of you, Easter, Passover, Thanksgiving, Valentine's day, and for countless other special calendar days, Mary never missed an occasion to send her "love and prayers" to family and friends alike. What never ceased to amaze me was her passion about each correspondence. Mary never sent a card without her personalization – an antiquated ritual long gone in this day and age of technological, non-personal messaging. For Mary, what was more important than the hand-selected appropriate card itself was on the interior of the left jacket of each card. There would be the inclusion of

Mary's personal message; handwritten in perfectly scripted, fluid, and graceful letters in the most beautiful penmanship ever to pen a card, a note, or a letter.

Postcards reached family and friends all over Westchester County from each new area Mary found herself intrigued by. As far as Mary was concerned, her fantasy tour could last forever. But would it?

"Our agent had us booked into all the colleges and all the famous ballrooms of the time," Joel Palmer wrote with the sense of pride that stems from the accomplishments and the knowledge that this cohesive group, whose musical talents were unmatched and unrivaled, were highly sought after by the finest of clubs for the enjoyment of the finest of ladies and gentlemen. Together as brothers, the men endured tight living quarter for over ten grueling years on the road, covered hundreds of thousands of miles, and performed in countless venues for thousands of fans. It was their time to hit the big time. But it was not to be. Their collective dream came to a screeching halt.

The band began to break up one musician at a time as each was drafted into the Second Great World War. Saul was the first to be called to duty. Angelo, Zum (Monk), Joel – one by one – summoned.

"It was disappointing to all of us when Uncle Sam called me into the Air Corp.," recalled Joel. "We were scheduled to appear in the Capital Theater on Broadway in New York City in September 1943. Instead, I was in the Pacific."

The disappointment of being so close and yet so far was agonizing and painful. But so, too, was the fear Phil confessed he felt for the safety of his family and lifelong friends. A piece of his heart was ripped out with each new draftee. "Everybody was going. My brothers, Pat and Henry, were called to serve in the Navy, and my nephews, Bobby, Richie, and Billy, were called to the Army. My band family, too. All of them were fighting for us. I wish I could have gone with them," Phil revealed. "I felt helpless. All I could do was to pray for all of them to come home safely."

There were several band members exempt from the draft – Phil due to his paralysis, Joe due to the accident and the pins still anchoring his ankles and legs, Hank due to a hernia, and Tommy due to poor vision bordering on legal blindness.

The once tight-knit band of brothers in the Vernon Troubadours and the Joel Palmer Orchestra had been Tommy's eyes as well as his guardians; taking care of him on and off the stage. But with the majority of the guys called to War and the four remainders in flux, Tommy found it increasingly more difficult to maneuver with his sight in continual decline. Phil was devastated when his best man opted to head home to Mount Vernon. Phil, Joe, and Hank decided to tough it out as long as possible.

As the War escalated, the bands dwindled, and leaders scampered to find replacements. With only a few guys left, Phil was ready to pack up and head home. But Mary was not. She had waited too long for the opportunity to see the world, and as exhausting as traveling was, she was not about to give that up so soon.

Years earlier, Phil had met a female bandleader named **Mary Marshall** in South Carolina. Not an instrumentalist herself, her main talent was her stature – "a 5' 6" pretty blonde" who was the leader of an eight piece all male orchestra. Intrigued by this assemblage, Phil, when asked, agreed to join the group.

Phil wired Marshall the details of his and Mary's arrival and requested transport from the train station. Having waited over an hour, a taxi was summoned. Upon arriving at the hotel, Phil checked the bandstand only to find his unopened telegram still sitting on the piano. Although Philly and Mary were leery regarding the lack of concern on the part of the leader, it was decided they would stay. They were in desperate need of cash, and this was an opportunity to earn some. The band was good, but in no way compared to the Palmer group. Still, Phil was working.

Several weeks flew by, and although the band played on, the dance would be quickly over. It happened one morning at two am. The band was still playing its' set when the hotel boss seized the bandstand, faced the audience, and bellowed, "O. K. That's all folks. Everybody out!" Turning to the startled members of the band, he ranted his directive at the musicians. "Everybody out! Get out! All of you!"

Phil leaned over to start packing up his horn when he caught a glimpse of the boss packing. Partially covered by his jacket, there was no mistaking the gun. Phil recalled, "I never got out of a place so fast in my life!"

A brief stint with the **Dick Shelton Orchestra** took the couple to Indianapolis, Indiana where the band entertained at the Gingham Gardens and broadcasted live from WCBS nightly. The admission to the Gingham Gardens cost a hefty one dollar per person with food and a drink included in that charge. From there it was a long trek to the Rainbow Room in Albany, New York. The gigs continued to see-saw.

As the War raged on and pulled from the ranks of the orchestras, Phil moved on to New Orleans, Louisiana where he joined the **Carvel Craig Orchestra**, a mainstay at the famous Blue Room in the Roosevelt Hotel. At the home of jazz, Phil was in his element, and Mary fell in love with her favorite of all the cities she had been to.

It was great while it lasted, but Phil felt the end was in sight. Mary's prayers were answered as one phone call changed Phil's premonitions.

"Is this Phil Keen?" an unfamiliar voice questioned.

"Yeah. Who's this?"

"It's Bill McCune. I need a trumpet man, and I hear you're the best!"

"Yeah. Who started that rumor?" Philip quipped as both men laughed.

Philly agreed to join the orchestra if McCune would also take a couple of other musicians. The deal made, Phil, Joe Tanno, and Hank Kass met up with the Bill McCune Orchestra. A popular recording group touted as **Bill McCune and His New York Orchestra** continued on tour with its newest members in tow.

At the time, Phil did not realize how successful the McCune group had been. He was just excited to be playing with such great talent and also with several of his West Side buddies from the Vernon Troubadours and the Palmer Orchestra.

Mary was elated to continue her whirlwind escapade. "It was the most exciting time of my life," she told me. It could have gone on forever as far as she was concerned.

Bill McCune, a sensational tenor sax man, had a top-notch group behind him – Phil, Moe, and Pete Rienze on trumpets – Bill McCune, Hank Kass, Ed Snapley on saxophones – Joe Tanno on bass – Bob Rogers on drums – and featured vocalists Peggy Steele and Tiny Morris to name a few members. "These New York guys were great," and audiences could not get enough of their swinging music. From the Lake

Club on the SE corner of Bunn Park, the band broadcasted on WCBS at 11:30 nightly. Dancing couples poured into the Club for sixty-five cents admission, tax included. The group moved to another favorite venue, The Beverly Hills Country Club in Newport, Kentucky, which boasted a cast of fifty performers along with the McCune ensemble. Mary and Phil were elated to be in the thick of the excitement of the extravaganza.

After several months, Phil received yet another call and an offer that seemed impossible to refuse.

"Is this Phil Keen?" Sounding similar to the call received from Bill McCune, the voice on the other end this time was the legendary Blue Barron. Billed as the music of Yesterday and Today, the **Blue Barron Orchestra** was a top recording group on the MGM and the Blue Bird record labels. Their recording of *Cruising Down The River* hit the top of the charts and sent the group sky-rocketing to fame. Considered one of the greats of the Big Band Era, Blue Barron received the top of the marquee status in every venue.

Was this the same Blue Barron that was on the phone with Phil? With his knees buckling from under him, Phil was awe struck. "Yeah." Phil paused as if trying to remember his own name. "This is Phil – Phil Keen".

"Great! I need a horn player, and I keep hearing your name mentioned as the best".

There was no joking comeback this time for Phil. This was a serious offer from the great Blue Barron. Phil was tongue-tied.

Leaving Phil no alternative but to agree, Blue asserted himself. "Meet me at The Palace in Anderson, Indiana by next Thursday. See you there."

"We'll be there!"

"Who's we?" Blue snorted.

"Me and my wife, Mary. We'll be there."

"No!" Blue blurted boisterously. "Wives are not allowed! Not even my wife – no wives! I will see you at The Palace – alone!"

Before Phil could catch his breath or reply to that command, the phone line disconnected. *Now what?* Phil questioned himself. *How can I leave Mary alone in Omaha, Nebraska? How can I leave Bill McCune? What do I do now?* One question after another racked Philip's head.

Upon hearing the news, Mary urged Philly to take this once in a lifetime chance. After all he would be playing with the one and only Blue Barron, and that was an opportunity that might not come along again.

"Besides," Mary unselfishly alleviated any misgivings Phil was experiencing, "I'll be fine here, and I'll continue to work. And all of my friends in the band will be here with me. You have nothing to worry about. If all goes well with Blue, I'll meet up with you in a few weeks."

With Mary's blessings, Phil Keen landed at the train station in Anderson, Indiana – alone for the first time in a long time.

From The Palace in Anderson the Barron band took to the stage at the Grand Theater in Evansville, Indiana. At the Lake Club in Evansville nightly admission was fifty cents, this time not including food or drink. Philip could not help remembering how much Mary loved Evansville when the McCune orchestra played there. A sense of abandonment tore at Philly's heart. *How dare I leave Mary alone in Omaha.*

Without Mary knowing it, Phil called McCune. "Will you take this old horn player back?" When receiving the answer he had hoped for, Phil Keen gave his two-week notice to the great Blue Barron and never looked back. For him, fame was not worth the separation.

Philip was back home with the McCune Orchestra, and all were delighted – especially Mary. The interesting part was that Phil was without question more in sync with the McCune Orchestra as this was a group of New York guys with tremendous talent. Before touring the country, the McCune group played at the Astor, The Plaza, and other famous New York City hotels. The band played swing music unlike the Blue Barron group whose music sounded sweet in the same vein as Guy Lombardo. In the Big Band Era, McCune's group with its New York roots increasingly gained notoriety as their on-air, live broadcasts were popular as were the recordings they made. Phil was in his element and loving it.

While at the Hotel Van Cleve in Dayton, Ohio, Phil decided to check out the USO across the street from the hotel. There appeared to be thousands of solders coming and going, and it piqued Phil's curiosity. Opening the door and peering in at the mass of uniformed men, Phil stepped inside for a closer look. Within four steps of entering the room, he bumped right into Anthony Carelli, an old buddy from his good old hometown of Mount Vernon. Each man could not believe the other was standing there. "Of all places to meet. What are the odds?" Philip looked back on that encounter with fondness. After countless hours and thousands of miles on the road, his Mount Vernon buddy brought a most welcomed spark of light to a weary traveler.

Throughout the year, a guardian angel must have been following the couple as they just missed several hurricanes, tornadoes, and floods either by a few days before the band arrived at their destination or a few days after they had left. In one close call situation, their luck prevailed. Late in arriving at one of the train stations, they missed their scheduled ride. The train they should have been riding derailed causing injuries and causalities among the passengers. They boarded the next train and prayed the entire way to their stop.

While in Pittsburgh in the dead of winter and the Christmas season fast approaching, Mary, Phil, and Joe Tanno decided to take a brief respite from traveling. They embarked on a cargo boat as the only three passengers. Eight hours later, the boat carrying their frozen bodies docked at the Port of New York. After a thawing three day respite, the refreshed trio returned to the band and continued their trek around the country.

16

And Miles To Go

Late 1943 – Early 1944

From the moment they landed in Richmond, Virginia, the newlyweds' hope of a restful honeymoon was anything but. There were miles to go with little sleep let alone peaceful rest. February, March, and April were frantic travel months – from The Tantilla Gardens in Richmond, Virginia to the Hotel Van Cleve in Dayton, Ohio to The Plantation Club in Dallas, Texas to the Hotel Peabody in Memphis, Tennessee to Lexington, Kentucky to Montgomery, Alabama to Biloxi, Mississippi to New Orleans then Shreveport, Louisiana to Omaha, Nebraska and finally to Springfield, Illinois.

The hectic itinerary ran into the May, June, July, and August schedule. From The Café Royale and The Palace in Anderson, Indiana to The Grand and The Lake Club in Evansville, Indiana. The group continued to Omaha, Detroit, and Lexington before a brief respite at the Hamilton Lake Inn in Hamilton, Indiana where the traveling ensemble swam and fished during the day and played their gig in the evening. Mary finally had a breather. She shocked everyone with her ability to swim like a fish, and Philly beamed with pride at having caught her.

It was the first time in months that the group could finally relax before the next series of dates took them to Battle Creek, Michigan then back to Detroit and on to Houston, Texas. The journeymen and their lady revisited the Palm Beach Café and The Lake Club in Detroit before they once again found themselves at The Hotel Peabody in Memphis.

The months from September through December brought the group to new venues as well as to favorite previous ones. From the Beverly Hills Country Club in Newport, Kentucky to the Argyle Hotel in Charleston, South Carolina to the Havelin Hotel in Cincinnati, Ohio to The Lake Club in Hamilton, Indiana to the Blue Moon in Oklahoma City, Oklahoma to Green's Terrace Gardens in Pittsburg, Pennsylvania to Ohio, Texas, Louisiana, and Texas – again.

After logging fourteen thousand five hundred sixteen miles, Mary and Phil celebrated their first year anniversary at the Blue Room in the famous Roosevelt Hotel in New Orleans. It had been quite a year of travel, and it was to be continued.

With full speed ahead, the Bill McCune and His New York Orchestra and Broadway Dance band toured far and wide adding to the already exhausting schedule. Among the countless sites traveled to on the tour, Phil and Mary each had their favorites.

One of Philip's favorite ballrooms was The Beverly Hills Country Club in Newport, Kentucky. What intrigued Phil most was the stage. When the orchestra was announced, the massive platform miraculously rose up from the underbelly of the building and moved forward out into the audience. The crowds went wild. So did Philip.

At the Veterans Hospital in Battle Creek, Michigan Philip lamented at the condition of the veterans there. After he played one of his many solos, Philly noticed a one-arm veteran clapping by slapping his one hand against his leg. Choked up, Phil thought of how he had to clap. Unable to hold up his left arm, he had to slap his right hand up against his left hand – but at least he had a left hand. Emotion overcame him. "I had tears in my eyes." And although he had difficulty containing himself, he had to continue playing. The veterans did their duty, and it was Philip's turn. It meant the world to Phil to make the vets happy even for the fleeting moment of one session.

Once again, the New York McCune guys landed at the Blue Room in the Roosevelt Hotel in New Orleans. Their one month contract kept getting extended as the orchestra gained a loyal following among the jazz crowd. Mary was totally enthralled by the city where music and people rocked in the streets all night long, and she later revealed that it was her favorite of all. The band ventured out to other locations then returned for renewed engagements. Musically, it was the place to be, but Mary would soon have to leave her beloved town.

Nearly two years into the chaotic yet exhilarating world-wind of road life, Mary became pregnant. An exhausting travel schedule was taking its toll on her energy, and it was agreed that she should return to Mount Vernon to set up house. It was not long before Mary found the couple's first apartment at 105 Mount Vernon Avenue. The apartment location on the main bus, truck, and car drag and its situation sandwiched between and above a local grocery store to the right of the entrance door and a shoe store to the left of the entrance door may not have been ideal, but for the forty dollars a month rent, it would have to suffice. Mary grabbed apartment 3A while it was still available. Residing next door in apartment 3B was Anna DeGloria, wife of Mike DeGloria who was in Europe fighting in the War. With so much in common, both women, left solo to tend to house affairs while their husbands were away, became fast friends – for the rest of their lives.

The rather large five rooms ran one into the other in a railroad car style reminiscent of the mode of transportation for the traveling musical ensemble. Longing to be back in New Orleans and on the road, Mary's comfort level in her new place slowly rose as the configuration of the apartment gave her the sense that she was still on board with the group.

Philly continued touring in a least twenty States, and in his thirteen years on tour covered upwards of two hundred thousand grueling miles aboard cars, buses, and trains. While in Davenport, Iowa he received yet another offer – this time to join the **Carmen Cavallaro Band** of stage and screen. About to appear in another movie, Cavallaro, dubbed the Poet of the Piano, needed a trumpet player to fill the spot of the one he lost to the War effort. *Hollywood, California! A movie!* What an incredible offer for the poor guy from the West Side of Mount Vernon. *Hollywood, California! A movie with the incomparable Carmen Cavallaro!* Just that thought sent Philip into a temporary tailspin. *But what about Mary? And the new baby to be? They will understand – won't they?*

Philip made his decision and boarded the next train.

The ride seemed like an eternity. Had he made the right decision? Philip's mind wandered to all of the places he had been so fortunate enough to see. The constant muted sound of the wheels on the track lulled him into a deep sleep.

"Next stop," belted the conductor so loudly that Philip's head hit the overhang as his body jolted up from his seat. Groggy and weary, Philip attempted to discern where he was.

The conductor realized that the dazed gentleman rubbing his head might miss his dismount. He stood by Philip's seat and bellowed again with an ear piercing resonance.

"Next stop – Yonkers, New York!"

Yonkers, New York never sounded so good, and Phil was overjoyed to be home at last. From the station he boarded the trolley to take him up Mount Vernon Avenue where he would finally see the apartment Mary had selected for them. As he entered the closet size foyer of the building, he focused on the one-inch black and white tile floor beneath his feet. One foot inside the foyer and to his left he noticed an entrance way that led directly into the shoe store attached to the apartment building. Since the store had a front entrance for customers, Phil thought the side entrance from the foyer of the apartment a bit peculiar. *Why is there a door from the foyer into the store? Who would ever use it?* he pondered. *The only people entering this area are the renters that live here.* With that thought left unresolved, he shrugged then continued to press on. Straight ahead of him was another door that led directly to the first set of vertical stairs towards the first floor apartments. Surveying further, Philip eyed the mailboxes to his right and that which he had been looking for – the individual apartment buzzers. He could not have been more excited. Mary had no idea that he would be coming home. With his right hand shaking, he pressed the bell three times to insure it would be heard.

"Who is it?" Mary yelled down from three flights up. "Who is it?"

"The mailman!" Philly playfully teased as he envisioned his wife wrinkling her forehead in confusion.

"Who?" she re-questioned with a curious yet cautious tone in her voice.

"It's the mailman!" Philip joked as he headed up the stairs towards the third floor.

It sounds like Philly, Mary contemplated, *but he's on the road heading west to California.* "Who is it again?"

"I have a special delivery for Mary!"

Mary started to cry. She was now certain of that less than perfect diction. It was her husband, and what a surprise special delivery it was.

17

Clothes Make The Woman

March 1943

With merely two months until her own special delivery, Mary was beginning to feel most uncomfortable; her tummy bulging even beyond what it was when she weighed in at two hundred thirty pounds. Not really concerned with the bulkiness of her condition, she knew, or least she prayed, the excess poundage would be lost after the arrival of the baby.

What was cause for concern was the lack of clothing fitting her rotund body. As high priced maternity clothes were too costly for her miniscule wallet, Mary found herself with only two outfits from her scantily filled closet that suited her condition. The one outfit included a black skirt with a stretch band waist that was nearing its elastic capability. As the belt tightened to the point of cutting off supplies to the baby, Mary slit the band for relief. *No one will ever know* she figured, as her long sleeve, button down the front smock stretched to the mid-thigh area covering the make-shift skirt repair beneath it. Luckily, Mary's second outfit was a bit more forgiving. The flower-patterned dress draped more like a moo-moo than the jumper that it was and thus afforded room for expansion.

Although in her seventh month, Mary continued through the end of her pregnancy to craft hats at the millinery factory on Bleeker Street.

Owned and operated by the Kraisky family, immigrants from Poland, Mary was the only worker fluent in Italian and the only non-relative in the group. She was the outsider – but not for long. In order to communicate and to survive amidst those that she felt were talking behind her back, Mary, who dropped out of high school in tenth grade, taught herself the essentials of the Polish language. They loved her for it.

With work six days a week, Mary was desperate for a few additional sets of clothes. Every evening she hand-washed the outfit she had worn that day. The following day, with the first ensemble still drip-drying in the bathtub, she wore the second of her two outfits. With the task of clothing rotation becoming a tedious chore, Mary felt compelled to ask for the only help she had ever asked for. So determined to be self-sufficient – could she do it?

Mary and her best friend Annie Errico, who I would later select as my confirmation Godmother, walked to Helen's house. Mary knew that Philly's sister, Helen, collected used clothing in good condition to send to family in Italy. For Mary, used clothes were as good as new clothes. Still she was in pain at the thought that she was reduced to begging.

"Let's go." Mary pleaded with Annie. "I can't do this."

"We've come this far. It'll be okay, Mary," Annie assured. "They're family."

With Annie's encouragement, the two climbed the four steps of the front porch hand-in-hand. Gingerly, Mary knocked at the door wishing she could have been anywhere else at that moment.

The door opened. Mary felt some relief at the appearance of Helen's daughter, Marion, who had been Mary's maid of honor two years earlier. Surely a maid of honor would help.

Marion, bewildered at the purpose of this unannounced visit, greeted the two close friends. "Hi, Mary. Hi, Annie."

"Hi, Marion," both women responded in unison as though the holding of hands made them one.

"Wow. You look great. How do you feel?"

"I feel good. I'm a little - actually a lot- bloated, but good otherwise."

"When's the baby due again?"

"In about two months – middle of May."

For what seemed to be forever, the conversation took a sudden hiatus until Mary cleared her throat enough to be able to speak.

"I know your mother collects used clothes to send to Italy." Mary gagged as Annie squeezed her hand in support. "Since I only have two set of clothes that fit me, I was hoping that I could borrow one or maybe even two dresses. I promise to take really good care of them."

With her voice cracking under the pangs of distress, Mary continued her plea. "I'll even have the clothes dry cleaned before I return them."

But before Mary could figure out where she would even get the money necessary to dry clean clothes, the universe caved in right on top of her confirming her worst fears.

"Oh," Marion lamented. "The clothes are already boxed and ready to be sent out to Italy. There's nothing I can do about that now. I'm sorry, Mary. Maybe in a few months we might be able to lend you a dress or two before they get boxed. You understand, don't you? The boxes are sealed already."

Mary dropped her head to hide the tears about to roll down her cheeks.

"Boxes can be opened and re-sealed," Annie angrily interjected on behalf of Mary who was fighting to keep from collapsing to the ground.

"Well, not these. They're ready for mailing. I'm sorry about this."

The door closed leaving Annie attempting to keep Mary upright. Half way down the block, Mary, openly weeping, felt her lunch spewing forth as the degradation of that incident squeezed the life out of her. Mary was close to hyperventilation mode. Annie pleaded with her to take deep breaths, but beyond that advice felt helpless to comfort her friend. For awhile the two stopped walking as Mary complied with Annie's suggestion. The deep breathing kept Mary from fainting, but not from crying the entire route home.

It was then that Mary firmly avowed, "I will never, **never, NEVER** ask anyone for anything ever again. My baby will go to college, and we'll do it on our own. I swear to you now, Annie, as God is my witness," Mary declared once again so that Annie and God both had clarity on her edict, "I will **NEVER** ask anyone for anything ever again – **as long as I live!**"

The experience as painful as it was made Mary even more determined to succeed on own, and from that day forward, she did. Her fire had been fueled.

The cycle of wash 1, hang 1, wear 2 ----- wash 2, hang 2, wear 1 again continued two additional months. With each roundabout, Mary's resolve strengthened; her declaration a mandate for the survival and preservation of her husband, her baby, and for herself. As years passed, many may have thought her stubborn and unyielding, but those closest to her were keenly aware that those barriers were in a sense her protection from want.

Mary would take great pride in never having to be humiliated ever again. Whatever she was yet to accomplish would be on her own merit.

18

And Baby Makes Three – Sort Of

May 12, 1945

Exhausted from her fifteen-hour ordeal, Mary finally felt relief from her labor. The agony was over - or was it?

"Congratulations, Mary", gleamed an exuberant Dr. Caprara. "You had a perfect, 6 ½ pound baby girl!"

Although the message was loud and clear, Mary thought she had temporarily lost consciousness. *Did the doctor say 'girl'? No – not a girl. Can't be a girl. It's not possible. It's not a girl.*

"She has an incredible amount of black hair. Definitely, Italian! She's absolutely adorable." Dr. Caprara pressed on with descriptions apparently only he was thrilled with.

"Here, Mary. Take a look at her. She'll be cleaned up and then you can hold her."

Mary turned her head away refusing even a glance. *She – Her – Girl – Not my baby.* Mary's blood pressure skyrocketed.

Still attempting to catch her breath and thoughts, Mary snapped, "No! I had a boy! I had a boy!" she hollered as though willing it so. "I had a boy!"

Mary had promised Pop that hers would be the first and only heir to carry on the Lucchini family name. She could never – would never –

renege on her word – especially to Pop. Her baby was a boy – definitely a boy.

Stymied yet not rattled by the outburst, Dr. Caprara calmly repeated the previously announced good news as the nurse dipped the newborn to show her off to the new mom. "There, see, Mary. You have a beautiful daughter."

It's not possible, Mary fretted. *The baby has a pointed head and is a girl. She's not mine.*

"You made a mistake," Mary's voice cracked with panic. "You mixed up my baby with someone else. I had a son. What have you done to my son?"

Mary felt the life being squeezed out of her and started to sob uncontrollably.

"You're exhausted and you need to rest now, Mary. You'll feel better after you rest," Dr. Caprara reassured as the nurse administered a sedative.

"I had a boy!" Mary screamed, "and I'm not leaving this hospital without him!" The outbursts waned as Mary fell into a deep sleep.

In the waiting room Philly and his shadow Tommy paced in anticipation of the news. Philip felt faint at the appearance of the doctor.

"Congratulations, dad!" Extending his hand to shake Philly's, Dr. Caprara delivered the news. "Mary and your new daughter are both doing fine."

"Daughter?" Philip questioned as though he misheard in his anxious state of being. "A daughter?"

"That's right. A beautiful baby girl."

Puzzled by Dr. Caprara's calm demeanor in the face of a baby mix-up, Philip needed clarification. "How's Mary again?"

"Mary had a very difficult delivery and seemed quite confused and upset. She kept insisting that she had had a boy and refused to even look at her daughter. We had to sedate her so she could rest. I'm certain that when she wakes, she will feel better."

Certain, Philip cringed. *He doesn't know Mary.*

Suddenly Philip felt Mary's heartbreak and disappointment. *Now who will carry the Lucchini family name? Mary should not have promised Pop – but she did. How could **she** – **me** – **us** – ever face Pop again?*

Dr. Caprara interrupted Philip's misgivings, "Mary will feel better after a good rest, and when she holds the baby, the two of them will bond," he assured.

If she holds the baby, Philip winced.

"Come on! What are you waiting for daddy?" Tommy tugged at Philly's shirtsleeve, "let's go see your new baby."

Philly and Tommy peered through the nursery windows. "There she is!" Tommy pointed to the bassinet with the Lucchini nametag – and the pink bow.

Still woozy, Philly could not help himself. "She has my nose!" he joked.

But what's that point on her head? No joke. She has a pointed head. Philip felt a rush of panic.

"What is that point? Why does she have a point on her head? What's wrong with her?"

"Oh! She's beautiful – just like Mary", Tommy sighed unaware of Philip's concern.

With his fist making a hammer-hitting motion, Philip contemplated aloud. "I'll have to clunk her on the head to get rid of that point."

"What are you talking about, Phil?" Tommy, at this stage legally blind for years, squinted through his massively thick glasses. "What point? I don't see a point."

"Right there," Philip gestured toward the area of contention. "Right there!"

"She's fine," chimed a third voice.

Philly and Tommy turned to find Dr. Caprara peering over their shoulders. "Once again – she's fine. Mary had a difficult delivery so we had to help pull the little girl along. In a few days, her head will take shape and the point will subside."

With a reassuring tap on the backs of both on-lookers, the doctor continued on his way down the hospital corridor.

The two men smiled at each other then began making faces at the little one on the other side of the glass. Amid the goggling, aaahing, laughing, and joking, Tommy posed the inevitable question. "What are you going to name her?"

Her? Neither he nor Mary ever considered a name for a girl.

Philip sucked in a huge gulp of air. "I've got it. How about Zeemagualean!"

"Zee – what?"

"Now listen carefully, Tom." Philip quite amused by himself slowly repeated the name emphasizing each individual syllable.

"Zee – ma – gua – lean."

"What kind of name is that?" Tommy snickered.

"It's a perfect name," Phil defended. "It sounds Italian, and it fits with Lucchini."

Tommy's face wrinkled trying to make sense out of nonsense. "Have you lost your noodles, Philly?"

"You should know by now," Philly kidded, "If there is one thing I'd never lose, it's my noodles."

Smiling from ear to ear and glowing from his own creativity, Philip proclaimed, "Yup. That's her name. It's got rhythm. Hear this – Zee – ma – gua – lean – ah – Lu – keen!"

"It's got rhythm, all right."

Both men in unison snapped in the style of a big band beat and sang out what was the coolest name on the jazz scene. "Zee – ma – gua – lean – ah – Lu – keen."

Each looked at the other, and in an instant, bent over with the type of laughter that hurts the ribs. Yes, it was funny. But would Mary be as hysterical?

19

And Baby Finally Makes Three

Mary was anything other than amused. *How dare Philly come up with a name for a girl? How could he make a joke at a time like this?* Incensed, she was even more resolute not to leave the hospital without her son.

Dr. Caprara and his staff were at a loss as to how to handle this difficult situation. It had been five days since the birth, and Mary remained in steadfast refusal to see her newborn. The more coaxing, the more Mary's back arched like a lioness ready to attack. The days seemed to blur one into the other – day six – day seven – day eight – and still no movement on the issue. Hospital records and receipts validate a stay of a nine day stand-off. There was only one option left - but would she go for it?

"Good morning, Mary," smiled Dr. Caprara as he approached the bed with some degree of confidence knowing what was up his own sleeve.

"What's so good about it?" Mary retorted. "Where's my baby boy?"

"Well, Mary, that's why I'm here today," the doctor began to explain. "Your little girl….."

"Not my little girl! I will have you taken to court for taking my little boy."

"Okay, Mary. Calm down so you can sign these papers for me."

"What papers?" Mary demanded to know.

"Well, after thirty years in this practice, I know a good thing when I see it. Your baby girl will grow up to be an incredible young woman someday. So sign on this line."

"I will not unless you tell me what I am signing." One could almost hear Mary's foot stomping under the blanket.

Dr. Caprara knew that he now had Mary's attention. Praying that his plan would not backfire, he laid it on the line. "Well, my wife and I have discussed adding to our family, and we want to adopt your baby."

Mary nearly fell out of bed. "What? You want to adopt my baby?"

"Absolutely. At least you will have the peace of mind to know that your daughter will be well taken care of. She'll have everything she needs to grow into the healthy, successful, beautiful young woman we're sure she will be."

If incentive is what the doctor was going for, he certainly hit the right chord. *How dare he think that I can not provide for my own child? I can make my own child successful! I don't need his or anyone else's help.* Just the thought of anyone even suggesting she could not do the job herself was enough to send Mary into a rampage.

"So sign right here," he challenged attempting to hand Mary the pen and paper that were on his clipboard. "She'll be our little sweetheart, and ...."

"Like hell she will!" Mary threatened as a week's worth of emotional turmoil gushed forth. "She's my baby!"

Dr. Caprara took a huge sigh of relief as Mary finally took the pointed head little girl in her arms.

20

The Ups And Downs

Mid 1940's – Mid 1960's

The point subsided, but the colic continued for six agonizing more months. Aunt Anna next door and Uncle Mike's mother around the corner became invaluable aides in the quest to soothe the hollering new addition. "As a baby, you drove me crazy," Yurtz admitted on more than one occasion. Forty years later, with a twinkle and a wink of his eye he reiterated then added, "And you're still driving me crazy."

A battle was waged over the name I should be given. Yurtz, with his overactive imagination, fought for the rhythmic Zee-ma-gua-lean-ah-Lu-keen. Tommy, who had been chosen to be my Baptismal Godfather, belly laughed every time he heard the name, and although the two buddies were in stitches campaigning for the ridiculous, the only vote that truly counted was, luckily Mary's. She elected: Barbara-Jo

"Barbara-Jo?" Phil's curiosity piqued. He attempted to decipher the origin. *It's certainly not an Italian name – not a family name – not even a common name. Maybe the 'Jo' is in honor of Saint Joseph who the family prayed for in daily rituals.* With viable explanations running out, he floundered, "How'd you come up with that name?"

"Well, while we were in South Carolina, there was a dancer at the club who had a daughter with that name. Remember? She was a sweet little girl and smart as a whip."

Phil shrugged at having no recollection. *There's gotta be more to it than that*, he surmised.

"Our Bobbi will grow up to be just as smart and will go to college to be a doctor or a teacher," Mary asserted.

"Bobbi?" Phil thought Mary's explanation now suspect. After a brief contemplation, he figured out what he thought to be her motive for her name selection. *That's it. Mary wanted a boy so badly that she was desperate to give a girl a boy's name!*

Regardless of the origin or the motive, the nickname Bobbi immediately replaced the formal original.

The apartment at 105 Mount Vernon Avenue was more than adequate for the three of us. The front door of 3A opened directly into the kitchen, which was large enough for Yurtz to teach me to cha-cha and to rumba when I got older. A cloth curtain surrounded the base of the sink in an effort to hide the pipes and cleaning products below. Circling to the right of the sink, sat a gas stove followed by a long window with a clothesline attached to a backyard pole. Beneath the window rested one of several apartment radiators perfect for scorching a hand or a thigh that accidentally rubbed against it. A freestanding white metal cabinet stood between the long window and a smaller second window. Stuffed in the corner was the most important appliance in our kitchen – the refrigerator, which was stocked with the finest Italian delicacies this side of Italy. A convenient built-in floor to ceiling storage hutch featured an upper section of glass panels, a shelf for small items such as the toaster, and a solid double door base. To complete the round-a-bout, a double set of ceiling to waist-high doors when opened revealed the infamous dumb-waiter. Every evening at five o'clock sharp, the wooden, double shelved open assemblage could be heard creaking its way up the shaft as the custodian below labored to pull the ropes that carried the heavy but still empty contraption up to the third floor. And like clockwork, Aunt Anna, who suffered terribly from severe arthritis and was basically housebound, would reach across the shaft and knock on our door to signal the arrival of the waiter. With the trash securely stowed on the shelves and lowered to the second level, a daily conversation ensued across the shaft. Many times, the neighbors one and two floors below would call up the shaft and engage in our community conversation. It was quite a set-up and one of my favorite apartment features. Mom's favorite was the red and white square block tile linoleum floor, which she selected and installed. Yurtz, of course, loved the refrigerator section.

A lengthy hallway led to the front of the apartment, which overlooked Mount Vernon Avenue. Although each room lay to the right of the hall, the hall was in essence part of each room. Two steps from the kitchen was the bathroom. Lacking a shower, the bathtub, resting on four ornate legs was the centerpiece of this tight but functional facility.

The living room, my bedroom, my parents' bedroom, and yet another living room, later to become my bedroom as a teenager, followed in sequence. Of varying room sizes, all had one thing in common – lack of closet space. Only two of the five rooms had a closet, neither one large enough for three winter coats. At that time, closet space was not an issue as none of the three of us had enough clothing to fill those minute enclosures.

With the exception of the front room which overlooked the truck traffic on Mount Vernon Avenue, each of the other rooms had windows with scenic views of the adjacent apartment building that was a mere five arms-length distance from our building. As a result of the proximity of the buildings and the lack of sunlight able to penetrate the space therein, the alleyway between the two apartments was often dark and foreboding. In summer, the air circulation, being non-existent, created a virtual sauna making it nearly impossible to get a decent nights sleep. We bathed in sweat.

The largest room in the front of the apartment had a second exit door leading to the building hallway. Beyond the door to its right and not more than five steps from it was an enormous window with iron fire escape set of stairs which zigzagged down the front of building insuring a quick route to safety if need be.

Some speculated that the entire structure housing six Italian families could have been moved directly from Naples to Mount Vernon without so much as losing a piece of garlic. Whether ascending or descending the staircase, the aromas emitted by each apartment permeated the halls and scintillated the senses. One could not help feeling ravaged upon entering this domain. Our apartment became a hub for musician friends to congregate after gigs – a place where all were welcomed to chow down on the late night feasts that never ended. No one ever left our house feeling hungry. Although steak and eggs were served occasionally, Italian cuisine was everyone's favorite fare. The gang wolfed down Mom's famous meatballs, while Saul devoured Phil's linguini oglio-olio and Uncle Tommy slurped the pasta e fagioli. Yurtz ate it all.

While Mom worked in the Pelham Manor Grand Union Supermarket as a meat packer, Yurtz, unemployed except for weekend club dates, took on the roll of Mr. Mom long before it became fashionable. As keeper of the estate – the man in the role of house husband – cooking became his forte. No one could brew a better cup of coffee or blend a tastier spaghetti sauce laddened heavily with garlic, parsley, and oregano. With Yurtz as head chef, there was never a need to question what was for dinner. His addiction to macaroni of all shapes and sizes was legendary, and he even composed a song, *Mambo La Pasta*, in dedication to his favorite meal.

Consequently, we ate macaroni at least five times a week, and would have eaten it seven times had Mom allowed us to. We had macaroni with garlic and oil – macaroni with gravy of the tomato variety – macaroni with butter – macaroni with meatballs or hot dogs – macaroni with cheese – macaroni with pork and beans – macaroni with kidney beans, peas, or garbanzos – macaroni with broccoli, spinach, or escarole. With Yurtz as the culinary creator in our kitchen, any edible could be deliciously pared with his much beloved macaroni, and because of that, our apartment became affectionately known as "One – Oh – Five - Spaghetti Drive!"

To remove himself from the monotony of daily household chores, Yurtz would cart me down the three vertical flights of stairs with the bar of the stroller clutched tightly in his right hand, his left arm dangling helplessly at his side. As the back two wheels of the carriage pounded each step, I was jolted up and down and side to side as though on an amusement park ride. The ride up the staircase was even more treacherous, as the back wheels of my limo slammed into the back of each step with the force of a racecar hitting the wall. Mom was livid when she discovered he was one-arming me up and down the stairs while in my buggy. Yurtz assured her that her fears of dropping the precious cargo down the flight were unwarranted.

Years of bearing the load of objects using one arm resulted in the muscles in that arm to bulge to the point of abnormality when compared to the lifeless other arm. It was as though he had pumped iron on only his right side producing an arm at least twice and possibly three times the size of the other. The disparity between the sizes of both arms caused his paralysis with self-conscientiousness, and for my entire childhood, he never left the house with a short-sleeve shirt.

But the right arm was solid, massive, and strong enough to lift a toddler or an elephant if needed be. And with all the miles accumulated through the years of jogging the Virginia beaches as he had done each day before sunrise, Yurtz had the legs and the stamina, asthma aside, to complete his missions. "Besides," he joked, "I have to get rid of that point on her head somehow!" Mom was not in the least bit amused and forbade the dangerous procedure.

Yurtz's escapades up and down the staircase continued for years without Mom's knowledge. Not trying to be defiant, it was simply the only way he knew how to maneuver the chariot and the baby together. He would never let anything happen to his darling daughter.

We were inseparable – joined at the hip. Where Yurtz was, so was Bobbi. All of his friends on the West Side knew and loved me. Uncle Tommy, although relishing Zee – ma – gua – lean – ah – Lu – keen, re-nicknamed me, "Ba – Ba – Lu." Even the policeman on the beat had his own nickname for a chubby tot – "Butterball." Each gentleman took turns wheeling, lifting, and tickling me, and I had a grand time as the center of everyone's affection. Yurtz was certainly the proud papa of a group of friends yet to have their own offspring.

But even for the most loving of fathers, a break from the everyday routine as househusband seemed to have clouded his thoughts and his judgment. He decided to take a few guys up on their offer to join a game of cards. They were not his best friends; not even good friends. "They were just a bunch of guys that hung out on the streets and said hello to each other." *One card game*. Couldn't hurt – could it?

21

Don't Bet On It

Gambling was a way of life on the West Side for my dad and his friends. "If you lived on the West Side of Mount Vernon, gambling was part of the neighborhood educational curriculum! It was all around us – the card games at home, on the corners, in the barber shops, and in the back rooms of social clubs. The three digit number was a constant topic of discussion, and we played with the same dream of the big hit that lottery players of today dream of. It was illegal, but ignored because it was so wide-spread and accepted." As Augie recalled, "It was amazing to hear the rapid quotations of the odds and what the exact winning dollar amounts would be on all the different combinations of numbers. The bookies, runners, and number store owners and players would be given an A plus in math if had been an education course!"

Yurtz was definitely a master with numbers. He could add sets and combinations of numbers with their corresponding odds faster than one attempting to press the on button on a calculator. The man was a wiz.

Boyhood gambling became the activity of choice for most youngsters. It started when the boys attended Nichols Junior High School and most probably before that. During lunchtime, the pre-teens found secluded corners around the outside of the school building on North High Street and pitched the dice in games of craps. In the winter, the boys were allowed to remain in the bicycle room during lunch, a perfect area inside to warm the hands of those pitching the cubes. Yurtz was in every game he could muscle into. In those days, the *steaks* were high, so to speak, as the winner of each game won the right to bite the sandwiches of all the others!

With changes in maturity and the prize, the gambling continued. The pennies lasted only a short while, as most of the boys did not have many of those, and I know Yurtz would have rather kept the food as the ante. "These were a great bunch of guys," he affirmed. "We had a lot of laughs, and it kept us out of trouble." Or did it?

A group of guys from Yonkers as well as Mount Vernon were engaged in a hot and heavy game down by the Bronx River Parkway where the two cities converge. Because the stakes were a lot more than sandwiches, pennies, or nickels, Yurtz sat quietly on the ground watching the games in progress. He admitted to me that he was actually just enjoying the non-stressful situation he was in, as the outcome of each game would not affect his already empty wallet. Being quite the mathematician and numbers expert, he viewed the open cards of the others and calculated what he would be doing had he had the money to join in. Then it happened. With police car sirens blaring and cops swarming the scene, the chase was on.

"Guys were running," Yurtz confessed. "So I ran too and hid behind a bush." As the chaos continued, "money was flying everywhere!"

This was the perfect opportunity to cash in. Well hidden from view, or so he thought, Yurtz peeked above the bush and began snatching the bills falling around him and stashing them into his pockets. As his luck would have it, a gentle but firm tap on his back stopped him dead in this pursuit of riches.

"All right, Phil," a soft-spoken, familiar voice uttered. "What are you doing?"

Turning to see his foe, Yurtz recognized the West Side policeman standing behind him. Yurtz attempted to explain that he had been watching not playing, but in either case, his story did not matter.

"Come on – hand over the money in your pockets, and let's go," the cop instructed as she shook his head in disgust at having to take a friend to the station.

Yurtz complied immediately and stepped into the paddy wagon with the rest of the culprits. The only concern Yurtz had was that his Pop, who stood on the corner of Mount Vernon Avenue and Bond Street daily, might see him on the way to jail. He stayed out of sight as best he could lest Pop see him through the back window of the van. Pop would have been furious and, more importantly, disappointed. Yurtz was mortified at the thought of disrespecting the person he loved more than anyone else.

At the station, Yurtz was reprimanded, fined twenty-five dollars which he had to borrow, and freed to leave. Just being at the station was punishment enough, but the imposed heavy fine added salt to his wound and fury to his wife.

It had been a few years since those incidents, and although still leery about gambling and getting caught, the urge to play never dissipated. With the invitation lurking and a break from childcare needed, Yurtz figured he could partake of a friendly hand or two.

But what about the three-year old? Yurtz knew he was in total and complete control of my every move, as all it took was *the look* that kept me in line. He was determined to play a few hands of cards with the guys. *It won't be a problem* he figured as he sat me down on a living room chair facing the television and explained that he was going out for a little while. "Don't move from this chair until I come back," he instructed. "O.K? I'll be home soon. Don't move!" Even at that tender age I was highly disciplined, and he counted on that. He closed the door and left.

In the middle of Mount Vernon Avenue between the blocks of Bond and Bleeker and next to Steve's Luncheonette was a rather questionable storefront, which one could enter only upon invitation; its content a well-known secret. The glass windows painted a solid, deep blue hid the interior card tables and the gamblers therein.

Yurtz joined a group of friends thinking he would be there only a short while, but time and money flew past him. *Maybe one more hand* he contemplated as the door opened and an unfamiliar form oscillated into the dark, smoke-filled room. A burly guy with a gut big enough to house five pounds of macaroni approached the first table where Yurtz sat. "I want in," he demanded slapping a thick wad of bills and a gun onto the table.

Even if the bills were counterfeit, the gun was not. Without a moment's hesitation, Yurtz leaped up vacating his seat. "I was just leaving," he announced as he quickly scrambled out the door leaving his hand of cards and his meager change on the table where he had been sitting.

It had been a couple of hours since he looked at his watch and realized I was still at home. Even to his amazement, there I sat in the same chair he had left me in, not having moved even so much as an inch. He let out a huge sigh. The baby was fine. But would he be?

Much to his chagrin, bad news traveled quickly to Mom's ears regarding the afternoon of gambling. In a huff, she stormed up the stairs getting angrier with each stomp of her foot on the next rung. Entering the kitchen, she slammed the door shut with such force the dishes rattled and one of her prized tchotchkes from Woolworth's Five and Ten smashed into slivers as it hit the linoleum. She was irate.

"What were you doing today gambling away the little money that we have? I work hard for every dime to try to keep us afloat, and you – you are out throwing it away."

Suddenly, it hit her. She had been so worked up about the gambling, her mind completely obliterated the more important issue – the baby. With her tunnel vision now widened, she went ballistic.

"Where was Bobbi today? Where was she when you were gambling? Where was my baby?"

Yurtz knew better than to attempt a cover up. He knew he'd better come clean or all hell would break loose. "She was home," he admitted up front.

"What do you mean – she was home? Who was with her watching over her?" Mom was fuming and becoming more enraged as she drilled him.

"Bobbi was home – ah – ah – ah – alone. I made a mistake, and I'm sorry."

Mom's rage hit ten on the Richter Scale. She mustered up all the strength she could to keep from choking him right then and there.

"Sorry? Is that all you can say – you're sorry? Bobbi could have fallen out a window for all you cared. Suppose there was a fire? No one would have known she was here. What is wrong with you? Are you crazy or just plain stupid? Are you crazy and stupid? What the hell is wrong with you?"

Yurtz was in no position to counter those rhetorical questions, and certainly in no position to comment further lest he cause Mary to foam at the mouth.

He realized he was wrong. He could have been dead wrong. He cried and vowed never to make that same mistake again.

22

It's All In A Days Work

1950's – 1960's

After the road and the War, it was impossible for Yurtz to find work. His skill was as a musician, and his paralyzed left side did not permit the range of options others may have had. Out of work for several years before becoming a school crossing guard at the corner of High and Oak Streets followed by policing the hazardous tri-section of Lincoln Avenue, Bond and High Streets, Yurtz's main job was taking care of me, hardly a profitable endeavor.

Chuckling, he confessed that he had considered self-employment by undertaking the illegal but highly lucrative racket of booking numbers. He concocted a creative, fascinating, and brilliant bookmaking ploy. The strategy involved music, the perfect cover up for a well-known local musician. With each three figure number represented by a trio of notes, the transactions could be transcribed onto sheet music. Under the guise of musical notations, the drafts of the world's lengthiest waltzes would elude and baffle the authorities – that is – until they caught on and caught him. With the threat of incarceration and the even greater threat and consequences of Mom's ire, it remained a thought rather than an action. Fortunately, Yurtz was better at cooking up macaroni than of cooking up schemes.

Mom worked as a meat packer in a chain store supermarket. At the Grand Union in Pelham Manor, New York, the long, exhausting hours of hard labor could rival the hard labor of those working on a chain gang. In spite of the grueling schedule and heavy work load, the payoff was barely enough for necessities, let alone frivolities. To add salt to the wounds of overworked hands in a minimum wage position, the job took its full toll. She was spent.

At that time, Mom had to do what machines do today. One of her main tasks was to slice, wrap, then hermetically seal individual portions of meat. To insure freshness, the clear plastic cellophane-like material covering each serving allotment had to be made impenetrable by tightly securing it with a heating element akin to an iron. With numerous burns on both hands, Mom finally got the knack of sealing but never completely the knack of preventing daily cuts and burns to her hands. Serrated and swollen fingers often prevented Mom from routine usage.

Another facet of Mom's daily chores was to fetch the meat from the basement freezer for packaging behind the first floor meat counter. For a woman of her then small size, I was amazed at her ability to lift and to carry the weighty trays of beef from one floor to the other. On one jaunt to the lower level, her feet slipped from under her on the sawdust that lay atop the cold, wet floor. She hit the concrete back first. The sudden downward motion jerked her head forward before it too slammed the deck. Mom's attempts to summon aid remained inaudible beyond the thick cement underground walls that surrounded her. Unable to move, she laid helpless on the wet, freezer floor, her body and mind frozen in time. She drifted in and out of consciousness and once revealed that she was certain she had been there over the weekend. With her sense of time and actual motion at a stand-still, she did the only thing she could do to help herself under those circumstances – recite the rosary. Whether it was the prayers is dependent upon one's belief, but for Mom, it was her saving grace. A co-worker realized that he had not seen her in well over an hour and questioned her whereabouts. The rescue commenced.

The ambulance arrived within minutes of her discovery. She was dazed but not so dazed to stifle her realization that hospitalization would cost that which she could not afford. Frantic about the fees, she refused to be taken. But the extent and severity of the injuries necessitated professional analysis and intervention, and before she could muster up the strength to kick and scream, the ambulance was on its way carrying its delirious passenger to the hospital.

Although the hospital stay was brief, the effects of the injury lingered a lifetime. In the aftermath of the accident, Mom's back would forever be a source of discomfort and/or writhing pain depending upon her activities and the weather. Years later she would suffer from debilitating arthritis in a hunched back she could not straighten up from. I never knew anyone else to have worked harder and suffered greater, and I certainly never knew anyone else as resilient and perseverant. Through it all, she continued courageously, and for many years was our sole provider.

Money was hard to come by. Every penny and each S and H Green Stamp counted. Religiously, Mom glued the stamps earned from the weekly grocery purchases into the company prepared booklets; meticulously securing the stamps of varying denominations onto the designated corresponding sections in the pamphlets. Dependent upon the particular item needed or wanted, varied numbers of pamphlets were required. It was a tedious yet necessary and rewarding task. As the booklets neared completion, the anticipation of the items we could receive free mounted. It was a hallelujah day when I received, compliments of S and H Green Stamps and Mom's perseverance, my first Smith Corona portable typewriter; an item, I used from high school through the first several years of my teaching career.

To supplement Mom's wages, Yurtz taught trumpet to various numbers of students. At one point in time there were eleven students on his weekly list. Traveling to their houses saved our neighbors from the torturous practices of fledging trumpeters. Among the many average students were those who stood out as exceptional talents. Noah DeFeo, the most gifted of Yurtz's protégés, was eventually awarded scholarships from The Eastman and The Julliard Schools of Music. Additional noteworthy talents included Jim Colassacco and Bob Nelson. Bob attended Lehigh University where he became a member of the trumpet trio section known as "the guts squad."

But not all students rose to greatness nor had the ability to do so. Some were good – others average – a few never progressed beyond elementary status. Yurtz had the uncanny ability to predict within minutes how a student would respond to lessons and the level of potential possessed.

"You either have it – or you don't."

Not many students had the "it" factor – only the elite few for that matter. There were times when Yurtz would reveal, "he can practice forever, but he'll never get any better. He doesn't have it."

Not in the business of robbery, this was a situation Yurtz could but never would take advantage of, discussing options with the parents to best suit their children's talents or lack thereof. Although he was in desperate need of cash, his suggestion to some parents to, "save your money," more often than not landed on deaf ears. Students, even those with "less on the ball" begged his further assistance; a testament to an easy going, mild mannered, encouraging and gentle teacher. Kids loved him.

Because of the eleven students under his tutelage, there were those who were certain our family was rolling in dough. That would have been the case had Yurtz been business minded and charged what he was truly worth. His modest fees were based solely on the particular family circumstances, and a one, two, or three dollar an hour lesson was typical. And if the aptitude were there but not the pocketbook, he would accept less. I know for a fact that he actually charged Noah's family a whopping fifty cents – plus a sandwich for lunch! Often times with sandwich consumed and belly satisfied, Yurtz taught Noah another half-hour on top of the hour previous to lunch. With fees such as that, the only dough we were rolling in was the macaroni we ate every night!

23

Play Me A Song

From the day of the infamous gambling escapade, Yurtz towed the line and towed me with him. And just as Yurtz revered his Pop, I revered mine. For that reason alone, it is neither a wonder nor a mystery that I followed in his footsteps as he had followed in the steps of generations before.

My life was forever shaped the day I played my first note on the trumpet at the ripe old age of two. It occurred when Yurtz held his horn to my lips, and when I blew a perfect "G", he quipped, "She's got it!" referring to the innate musical talent of the Lucchini family.

I made my solo stage debut at the Bronx Winter Gardens – Bronx, New York at the ripened age of seven years. In the glaring spotlight, my tiny silhouette was dwarfed by the massive stage and glittered curtain backdrop. With the confidence of a professional, I took my stance, my dad's posture evident in mine. After all, I was his mimic, and if he played bell angled to the floor, I did likewise. Add to that the fact that, at seven years old, I simply did not possess the arm strength necessary to hold the weighty implement upright.

But the reality was and still is that no matter what stance I would ever take, I could never musically come close to the galaxy Yurtz inhabited. Not in this lifetime – not in any lifetime. The consummate musician was light years ahead of his nearest competition. In point of fact, musically, he had no equal.

Nonetheless, I did my best to shadow my idol. I belted out *Rock Around The Clock*, and with the acoustics in my favor, blew the house down. The guys in the band rose to their feet as did the entire audience. As band leader, Yurtz was in the pit being congratulated by his back-ups. "I told you she's better than me!" he boasted as he wiped the tears streaming down his cheeks.

Out in the assemblage of show-goers, Mom was in full-blown hysteria busting to present me with my first nosegay. Instinctively, I curtsied then threw several kisses out to the assembled, a gesture that became my signature every performance after that.

As a third grader I was invited to join the Hamilton Elementary School band under the direction of Mrs. Kaiser. Sharing Uncle Johnny's old horn proved at times to be problematic. Although a responsible kid, I occasionally and inadvertently neglected to bring the horn home from school. The custodians needed to be commandeered to open the building allowing Yurtz access to the horn for his weekend club dates.

With two years of experience under my belt and playing lead trumpet at Hamilton, I faithfully rehearsed my music in the front living room overlooking Mount Vernon Avenue, and even from three rooms away, I could not escape Yurtz's fine tuned ear to my every clinker.

"B Flat - first valve."

It never ceased to amaze me how he knew my every flaw then disseminated the corrections while watching television at the same time.

"G Sharp – valves two and three."

"Hold that note in measure five for the full four beats."

"Sit up straight. Don't slouch."

"Correct that rhythm – one, two, e, and, ah, three, four."

"Staccato not slur those notes in measure eight."

"Watch the key signature."

Our apartment was the Mecca for melody, and Yurtz, like the Pied Piper, had many tag-a-longs; Vinny next door, his number one follower after me. Aunt Anna and Uncle Mike were blessed with a new addition of their own, and I could not have been more thrilled at the arrival of a new playmate. From the day Vinny was brought home, we were inseparable. With a year and a half between us, we grew up as brother and sister, each being in the other's apartment so often that both sets of parents could have sworn they each had two children.

One of our deepest connections involved music. A rather naturally talented Uncle Mike, who dabbled at the guitar, could have been a great musician had he had the time to study his instrument. He played beautifully when he did play, and he became the catalyst for Vinny to take up guitar as his instrument of choice.

Yurtz had tremendous influence on Vinny and me, as we were surrounded by all genres of music every minute of every day. Many times we jammed together; Vinny on guitar, me on trumpet or vocals, and both of us under the watchful eye and perfect-pitched ear of Yurtz. He corrected notes and chords on the guitar as easily as on the trumpet, and we were in awe of his natural capabilities.

Although I relished jam sessions with Vinny for their pure enjoyment, these gatherings ultimately took a back seat to the cultivation of our technical knowledge and instrumental proficiency. For Yurtz and me, practice, as essential as breathing, was a mandatory part of our everyday routine. Lasting of upwards of two hours between us, the discipline involved in keeping the lips in condition was unyielding; especially for Yurtz whose half embrasure was still a source of anguish. Lip drills, excruciatingly painful and most boring for bystanders, were a must in our daily ritual. Although I pitied the poor neighbors every time I began a session, drills were a necessary evil. Then it was the master's turn. Not to disturb the neighbors any longer than necessary, Yurtz played standing in the closet, the bell of the horn pressed deeply into the coats in order to muffle the sound.

There had not been any complaints until Eleanor moved in below us. Although generally a personable, sweet Italian lady, her less than tender vociferations resonated throughout the neighborhood, especially when calling her son, Anthony. Eleanor bellowed in a singsong style, the notes of which Yurtz could easily mimic on the trumpet. When her bassoon-like roar summoned, "Eeeeeeeent – aaaaaaahh – kneeeeeee!" the compression of air was so forceful it set off a sonic boom that shook our building structure. As blaring as our trumpet practices may have been, they were mild in comparison. Anthony raced home from where ever he had been within the four square mile range of audibility.

Yurtz's practices were methodical and progressive – lip drills followed by a section of a melody, returning to lip drills. For the duration of his exercises, lip drills interrupted each song. One day as Yurtz repeated his usual pattern, a thunderous assault on our apartment stopped his concentration.

"What is that?" I contemplated aloud.

Yurtz shrugged then continued unconcerned with the minor interruption. But, once again, the cannons fired.

"What is that?" I re-questioned expecting an explanation this time.

"It's Eleanor downstairs," he accommodated. "She's hitting the ceiling with the end of the broom again."

Expressing her displeasure, our floor vibrated from the hits, and all attempts to continue practicing were stifled.

"What a witch," I snapped, "using her broom to aggravate us. She should use her broom to fly away."

Yurtz's spin on the situation was far different from my witch on her broom interpretation.

"Eleanor must not be feeling well today," he surmised. "Guess I'd better quit it for now." As Yurtz stepped out of the closet and removed the mouthpiece from the horn, the bombing subsided. It seemed as though a cease fire ordinance had been made from ceiling to floor. An eerie quiet descended on the apartment as Yurtz secured his peace disturbing weapon in its case. But the coast was not quite clear just yet.

The siege suddenly and unexpectedly exploded once again as Eleanor, leaving her broom on the second level, stomped up the flight of stairs and rammed her fist against our door. "Hey, Philly. Open up. Open up."

Pounding the door with the force of a heavy weight world champion boxer, Eleanor continued her assault on our door, I half expected her to threaten, *I'll huff and I'll puff and knock your door down!* With his prevailing cooler head and calm demeanor in the heat of battle, Yurtz complied with Eleanor's command and opened the door.

The dominate combatant stood her ground. "Hey, Philly. You're driving me to drink."

In an effort to restore harmony, Yurtz softly greeted his feisty opponent. "Hi, Eleanor! Listen, I'm sorry if ...."

"No! You listen!" Eleanor reprimanded as she interrupted Yurtz's grovel at an attempted apology and amnesty. "Enough, already!"

Eleanor's gruffly voice echoed off the hallway walls amplifying it to decibels which damaged the eardrums. "When the hell are you going to finish a song?"

"I know the horn is loud," Yurtz appeased, "so I play in the closet to ...."

"I don't give a damn where you play! When the hell are you going to finish a song?"

Yurtz was stymied for a few moments until the realization of her demands hit him head-on. "What? Finish a song? Your mean – you're not mad at the practices? You just want to hear a song all the way through?"

Eleanor gestured the approval of his final analysis of the problem. With that cue, Yurtz unloaded his noisemaker and gave a command performance for one. With Eleanor's choice of melody completed, all peace was restored. A subsequent truce commenced with the condition that Yurtz would end each practice session with a full version of a song dedicated to Eleanor.

That may have satisfied Eleanor, but not me. In my mind's eye, if Yurtz would dedicate a song to **her**, then he had better do the same for his most adoring fan – his only daughter – **me**. From that day forward, whenever Yurtz played a club date, I put in my request, "Play ME a song, Daddy." Invariably he acknowledged with his characteristic nod and twinkling wink, and invariably I repeated, "Play ME a song."

Angelo and Santa (Groccia) Curto
Grandpa and Grandma Curto

Felice and Marianna (Petti) Lucchini
Grandpa and Grandma "Toot-Toot"

1932
Citizens Concert Band
Grandpa "Toot-Toot" On Sousaphone

1930
A Young Phil Keen
Following In His Father's
Footsteps.

1932
The Vernon Troubadours

Norm Kelly, Tommy Castelli, Joel Palmer, Tony
Mongarelli, Angelo Greco, Philip Lucchine

1933

The Vernon Troubadours

Tony Mongarelli, Phil Keen, Joel Palmer, Norm Kelly, Tom Castelli, Hank Kass, Angelo Greco

1934

The Vernon Troubadours

Phil Keen, Tony Mongarelli, Tom Castelli, Joel Palmer, Hank Kass, Norm Kelly, Angelo Greco

1938

The Joel Palmer Orchestra

Front: Joel Palmer, Hank Kass, Angelo Greco, Saul Vinokur
Back:　Phil Keen, Tony Mongarelli, Tommy Castelli, Joe Tanno

1939

The Joel Palmer Orchestra
Lawrence Inn – Mamaroneck, New York

Angelo, Joel, Saul, Joe, Tom,
Inn Owner, Tony, Hank, Phil

Tom, Saul, Phil, Joe,
Hank, Angelo, Joel, Tony

1940

The Joel Palmer Orchestra

Phil, Tom, Tony, Joe, Joel, Vocalists Bill Virga
and Jimmy Dee, Hank, Angelo, Saul

1941

The Joel Palmer Orchestra

The Tantilla Gardens – Richmond, Virginia

Front Row: Joel, Saul, Angelo, Hank, Vocalists
Carol Enders and Bill Virga
Back Row: Tony, Phil, Pete Rienzi, Joe Tommy

1941

The Joel Palmer Orchestra

The Tantilla Gardens – Richmond, Virginia

1942
On The Road

1942

A Swinging Courtship

February 7, 1943

The Wedding Of Phil Keen To Mary Curto

1943

Dick Shelton Orchestra
Indianapolis, Indiana

Soloist Phil Keen
Rehoboth Beach
Country Club, Delaware

117

1943

On The Road With Mr. and Mrs. Keen

New Orleans, Louisiana

1944

At The Home of Jazz
New Orleans

119

February 7, 1944

The Keen's First Anniversary and Phil's Birthday
Texas

May 12, 1945
And Baby Makes Three

1952

The Bronx Winter Gardens – Bronx, New York

Bobbi-Jo
Age 7
Following In Her Father's Footsteps

1960's

The Nick Marra Orchestra

Glen Island Casino – New Rochelle, New York

Phil Keen On Trumpet Flanked By
Vocalist Gracie Dell and Nick Marra

1960's

The Nick Marra Orchestra

Bordewick's Dining and Dancing Club
Tuckahoe, New York
Front: Norm Rosner, Saul Vinokur, Nick Marra
Back: Phil, Bill Fafley, Nick Luiso, Pete Hunt, Joe Tanno

Glen Island Casino
New Rochelle, New York
Bill Fafley, Phil, Mike Piazza

July 4, 1981

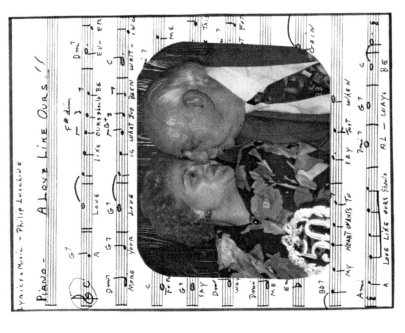

24

Mother Knows Best

1957

Yurtz was quite confident that he had one up on Mom, but she would not be denied the pleasure of spoiling his perfect record in that category.

Unbeknownst to me, upon the completion of one of our daily practices, Yurtz inadvertently left the horn on the chair. Not seeing the horn, I plopped myself down right on top of it. Seemingly unharmed, Uncle Johnny's old horn was placed back in its case and taken to school the following day as per usual. Much to my horror, as our band rehearsed for the spring concert, the trumpet broke in half in my hands. As I sat holding a piece of horn in each hand, members of the band thought it quite comical. But, for me, this was no laughing matter. I was traumatized. Yurtz, however, took the incident in stride, and with his calm demeanor and "it's no big deal" attitude, he attempted to tape the pieces together. With an entire roll of black tape strewn around the instrument, Yurtz tested his mended piece of modern art.

"There," he proclaimed nodding his head confidently like Stan's partner Ollie. "It's as good as new!"

But like the predicaments of a favorite comic duo, this situation could not have been any further from reality. The tape slowly unraveled as we painfully watched our horn rendered useless. Another nod akin to Ollie and Yurtz solved the dilemma yet again. With a school-issued horn, the spring concert commenced as did Yurtz's weekend club date.

Even with the stigma of a school-borrowed horn, Yurtz was hesitant to purchase a new one. But for him, a horn was not a luxury. It was his lifeline. Nonetheless, Mom had to drag him kicking and screaming to Rosner's Music Store in Yonkers, New York where he finally purchased his very first shiny new instrument. But just when Yurtz had thought the shopping spree had ended, Mom hit him with a crazy suggestion. "Let's buy one for Bobbi."

"A trumpet for Bobbi?" Yurtz could not believe his own ears. "We can't buy her a new horn too," he cautioned as his mind quickly worked overtime to come up with a good excuse he knew he needed in a hurry.

"And why not?" Mom retorted with total confidence that he would not be able to successfully argue against her.

"Well," Yurtz protested, "she will never play past sixth grade. She's only going through a phase, and she'll forget all about the trumpet when she gets to junior high school. You'll see."

"No. You'll see," Mom asserted with certainty. "She loves to play, and she will continue to play."

Hard pressed to find a point he could win, Yurtz blurted emphatically, "No, she won't – because she's a girl!"

"A girl?" That hair-brain reason only served to fuel Mom's fire. "A girl? And just what does that have to do with it?"

Laboring to get himself out of the hole he had just dug, he explained his rationale. "Girls don't play this type of instrument. When she gets older, she will not want to be the only girl in the trumpet section and maybe the only girl in the whole brass section." Feeling rather confident in his reasoning, he added, "She's a girl, and she will quit – mark my words!"

But no one's words could ever be marked like Moms'. From the day of the dress incident, she became obsessed with obtaining the essentials of a good life for her family. And a trumpet for her talented eleven-year old, no matter the gender, was, in her estimation, worth the financial struggle to achieve her goals.

Although she had promised Pop she would have a son, she nonetheless beamed with every accomplishment of her daughter letting Yurtz know that in no uncertain terms.

"You should be proud to have a daughter – a girl – who can play the trumpet as well as she can!" The intonation of her voice suggested that she was proud, and how dare he not be.

Yurtz's buttons had been pushed way too far on that note. "I am proud of her," he snapped, his tone in compliance with his anger towards anyone who would even dare to suggest otherwise.

"Maybe a son would never have played the horn," Mom speculated. "How blessed we are to have a girl who does."

The tension of the argument dissipated as both realized the tug of war was over. With steadfast persistence, Mom finally won the standoff with points that made more sense and were hardly arguable.

"Well," Yurtz conceded jokingly, "she does play better than me. Guess she should have her own horn."

Money was extremely tight, and although there was not extra for frivolous items such as a new trumpet for me, a deal even my dad could not refuse was made with his dear musician friend and storeowner, Norm. My present was to be locked safely away in Norm's shop and paid for a few dollars at a time. I was oblivious to this arrangement, and since I would not dare touch my dad's new Selma from France, I happily continued playing the old school horn throughout the summer and into the next school year.

Time moved swiftly by. I was in sixth grade. With our holiday concert over and vacation on the horizon, I was excited to see what 'Santa' would bring. Christmas day finally arrived, and I enjoyed opening my usual gifts – pajamas, socks, underwear, a sweater, and a skirt. I was always happy and quite satisfied with whatever 'Santa' brought me, which was certainly more than what my parents had received when they were youngsters. I hugged and kissed my parents to thank them for the gifts I could not wait to wear. With a twinkle in her eyes brighter than all the lights on our tree, she pointed out that I had not opened all my gifts. There hiding behind the base of the tree was yet another gift. I sat on the floor and leaned over to see what she was pointing to – a strangely shaped orange, brown, and black speckled case. I felt faint. Could it be? As I pulled the case towards me, I was already crying. It could only be one thing, and I could hardly contain myself. I started to shake and required help opening the latches. The top lifted, and there it was – my very own shiny, new trumpet. Through the tears I could not believe my own eyes. It seemed like it took forever, but reality finally set in. I had my own horn, and my most memorable Christmas ever.

Mom could have reveled in an 'I told you so', but she never had to. She was right all along, and all of us knew it. Yurtz was happy she had talked him into a trumpet for me, especially when I played with him and the guys in his bands.

Although by the age of twelve, I had played with most of the regulars in the various bands Yurtz played in, the newcomers, invariably surprised by my performances, would delight in teasing the master. "Hey, Phil. Who needs you anymore?"

And with a grin wider than the Grand Canyon, Yurtz acknowledged his musician buddies. "Yeah. I told you she plays better than me."

"And not only that, Phil. She's better looking than you! She's got your talent, but luckily not your nose!"

In reality, with my mother's nose and one-one zillionth of a fraction of my father's talent, I was definitely the lucky one.

25

On The Road With The Youngest Keen

Like the generations of Lucchinis before me and with my new prop in hand, I began my own traveling career. I auditioned for and was selected to become a part of the Police Athletic League's Talent Group. At age twelve, I was the youngest and the only instrumentalist in a group of teenage singers and dancers under the direction of Mada McEntyre, music teacher at Our Lady of Victory School in Mount Vernon. Community groups throughout Westchester County sought our highly rated shows. The Westchester Womans Club was our number one venue, and although most of our shows were presented at that facility, we did travel to various clubs around the area. For two years I enjoyed life on the road on the weekends, but for reasons unbeknownst to me, the group broke apart in 1958 with a culminating performance and awards banquet.

After a twenty-five minute train ride from Yonkers, we arrived in New York City where, at the age of twelve, I auditioned for the *Ted Mack Amateur Hour* show - television's original *Star Search* and *Americas Got Talent*. As with the more recent versions of talent shows, the viewing audience selected each week's winner and the one to continue competing to the finale. While Mom and my dad's sister,

Rose Reisman, sat anxiously in the waiting room, Yurtz and I entered the make it or break it room. After Yurtz gave a few directions to the pianist, I belted out my rendition of *Rock Around The Clock*. Several of the other hopefuls waiting their turns in the contestant's area jumped up and danced the lindy; a scene Mom and Aunt Rose said they would never forget. As I played flawlessly into my second chorus, I gained the confidence I needed to do my signature move. While playing and holding the horn in my right hand, I hammed it up with my left hand swinging and snapping to the beat – hips swaying. The judges smiling and nodding to the steady rhythm marked their approval. I knew they were hooked.

Requested to wait in the main room for the judges' final decision, Yurtz and I stepped back into the contestant's area whereupon a standing ovation erupted from all who were there. After a short delay, we were called back to the judgment room. Waiting our arrival were the papers Yurtz and Mom had to sign to allow a minor to appear and to compete on the show; the date and time to be later determined. With excitement beyond any that had been felt before, the four of us left sky-high on a cloud that did not come down for weeks.

But weeks turned into months with no further word about my appearance date. As had happened many times with my father's attempts to have his music published only to be told Rock was in and his sentimental style out, my cloud, like his, would eventually burst too. Perhaps it was the show's hiatus or the changes of networks it was experiencing, but I was never contacted to appear. Like father – like daughter in so many ways.

But also like mother – like daughter. I would never let one disappointment stop me from doing that which I loved. My career continued.

In the last class of the day, I sat by the window in Nicholas Junior High School. From there I had the perfect eye's view of the A.B. Davis High School marching band practicing their maneuvers on the stadium field behind the back-to-back schools. It was mesmerizing, and I could hardly wait my turn to be part of that organization. My day came at last, and as I stepped into the band room at the high school for the first time, I felt my heart and nerves racing out of control. Everyone, including newcomers, seemed to know their place. Taking their cues, I sat on the last seat in the trumpet section. *Where else would I be seated?* I questioned myself. *There are eleven guys better than me,* I conjectured, *so I guess I belong in the last chair.*

The music director, C. Andrew 'Doc' Randall, came bounding into the room, his booming voice overshadowing the one hundred noisemakers playing nonsense on their instruments. I looked up at the source of the overpowering vibrations and was stunned to see a lean, slightly built dynamo bellowing before me – his deep blue eyes glistening like the Mediterranean. It was Doc all right. With the exuberance, energy, and excitement of a three-ring circus rolled up into one man sporting the biggest smile I had ever seen, my adoration towards him was immediate. At the time, I was rather introverted, and although I practiced my parts to the point of mastery and memorization, I remained quietly in the background as the freshman of the trumpets.

Without my knowledge, Noah DeFeo, my dad's premier trumpet student and first chair leader of the section, had mentioned my name to Doc. "Do you know who that girl is in the last seat of the trumpets?" When Doc confessed he did not know me, Noah proceeded to inform him. "Her name is Barbara-Jo Lucchine. She's the daughter of my trumpet teacher, Phil, and she can play that horn. Right now her talent is not being used where she is. I've heard her play, and I'm telling you – she's good." Doc undoubtedly made a mental note and would soon test Noah's assessment.

During this same period, one of the members of the trumpet section, who had been arriving to band rehearsals late, tested Doc's patience one too many times. Doc seized the opportunity to audition me in front of the entire band. "Charlie. This is the fifth time you are late." Since being late was not a violation of any musical laws, Charlie was confident he was still in the good graces of the maestro. But much to everyone's surprise, before Charlie could get comfortably situated in his normal third chair position, Doc redirected him. "Change places with Baaah-bra." I was stunned as I had no idea Doc even knew my name.

Charlie gave Doc the *are you kidding me* look, but Doc was not laughing. "You heard me. Change places with Baaah-bra."

The room, normally blaring with instrumental activity, was dead silent, and I sat motionless as Charlie reluctantly started to move in my direction; all ears and eyes glued on the proceedings. "Baaah-bra, please take Charlie's chair. Leave your music and take his third seat."

I was mortified from the unwanted attention, and although I complied, I felt like the tiger's prey, as Charlie's ire was displaced towards me. If mere stares could have killed, I might not have been alive today to retell this story. It was not until weeks later that I realized the rivalries and competition for seat placement was so fierce.

Doc pressed on, his arms waving frantically to keep the beat and the instrumentalists in sync. When the components failed to mesh, as was the case quite often, Doc stopped the group to re-focus on the composer's intent. To make necessary corrections and adjustments to difficult portions of the music, it was normal for Doc to request particular instrumental sections to play their parts without the interference of the band back-up. It was during one of those breaks that Doc challenged the trumpet section. I was shaking in my loafers, as, I, in essence, would be sight-reading my part. Noah leaned towards me and encouraged, "Take it easy. Play like I know you can."

Doc raised his arms, and the eleven of us in the trumpet section lifted our horns in response to the conductor's command. I sucked in all the air around me and began on the downbeat with the rest of the horn players. As the difficulty level of the piece rose, players dropped out one by one. Noah, who could play his first chair cornet part blindfolded, bowed out in an effort to ensure that Doc could hear me. I was so immersed in my part and riveted on Doc's direction that I was not cognizant of being the only trumpeter still playing. Apparently my solo performance continued for quite awhile, until it finally dawned on me that no one else was blowing their horn. I immediately stopped mid-measure and waited for the inevitable public critique. Doc's facial gestures telegraphed his elation before his words. "Well," he announced, "I finally have a good trumpeter!"

With the exception of Noah who was gloating at his prior assessment, the guys were miffed. The very idea that a girl could play at all, much less better than they could, was too much for their male egos to handle. Fortunately, of the eleven males, at least eight of them were my dad's students, and when they discovered my link to their beloved teacher, they befriended me. Even Charlie, who was reinstated to his original first cornet position, became a friend. I was moved to first trumpet fourth chair – then third chair after Charlie graduated.

On May 12, 1962, Bob Nelson, Charlie, and I performed a trumpet trio of the famous *Carnival of Venice*, ours a complex version Doc insisted that we memorize. Before our performance, as if my nerves were not already getting the best of me mentally reviewing my part, Doc made a surprise announcement that sent me over the edge. Instructing me to stand alone, he revealed that it was my birthday and led everyone in the packed house in singing *Happy Birthday*. I was a wreck by the time I took my position with Bob and Charlie, the three of us standing in front of the band. With that set of twinkling blue eyes and gleaming grin, Doc had pulled off an unforgettable moment in my life and one that I have cherished ever since. I engulfed enough air to allow me to play the entire piece without another breath should I have required to do so. As I looked to Doc for the downbeat, his beautiful face gave me the encouragement I needed at that moment. I made it through for myself as well as for Doc, a special person who will always hold a place in my heart.

The years in the A.B. Davis High School band, orchestra, brass choir, and conductor's club were some of the best years of my life. Our marching routines were second to none, and we were noted for our letter formations during football pre-game and half-time shows. With the exception of two shows that were repeated due to popular demand, our half-time spectaculars varied each week and consisted of letters, various formations, and even dancing and singing routines while playing music specially selected to compliment the maneuvers we performed. To me, this was serious business, and although it required countless hours of preparation, it was a tremendous source of pride.

During high school and college, I performed with the Mount Vernon Municipal Band, which was under Doc's leadership. Our summer concert series was a popular community event as crowds gathered in front of City Hall every Tuesday evening for top-notch entertainment on steamy summer nights. Regardless of the summer production, such as *The Mikado* featuring the lead vocalist, Vivian Randall, Doc's wife, I was on call whenever Doc needed a trumpet.

At SUNY – Oswego, I played for sorority events, the most exciting one being my solo performance in the campus-wide annual float parade.

With the theme of the parade being music, our sorority selected to highlight the blues genre. I stood front and center on our float, and as it proceeded along the parade route from the campus through the main area of the town, I knocked out *The Birth of the Blues* on my horn – live and in person.

Although I earned a degree in science, I continued my musical adventure playing for high school musicals including *The Pajama Game, Guys and Dolls*, and *Fiorello*. In community theatre groups I played in the pit for *Carnival* then on stage in the musical *Gypsy* where I received an award for my interpretation of *Mazeppa*, the singing and dancing stripper who can "bump it with a trumpet."

One of my greatest achievements occurred at the Post Lodge in Mamaroneck, New York. It was 1968, the year of my college graduation. Yurtz asked the guys in the band if I could sit in for one number. Having been away at school, I had not yet met any of these particular musicians nor had they any inkling that I could play the horn. Out of respect for Yurtz, the musicians reluctantly agreed to let me join them on the bandstand not quite knowing what to expect. I smiled and nodded hello as Yurtz introduced me to the group. "This is my daughter, Barbara-Jo. I'll let her take it from here."

Yurtz stepped back and motioned that I had the floor. Taking my cue, I began disseminating pertinent information regarding my solo. "I'll play *Cherry Pink and Apple Blossom White* – key of B Flat – moderate cha-cha tempo. After the first four notes, everyone will stop playing as I slur slowly to the fifth note like Prez Prado. I'll play that for each of the sections."

As I spoke, I noticed a few looks of disbelief; some guys looking back at my dad then back to me. Unaffected, I continued. "I'll play the entire song once through." Pointing to the alto saxophone man, I directed, "You play the next two choruses. I'll come in again in the mid-section and finish up."

"Okay, boys," the pianist interjected. "You heard the lady. Let's play it."

Giving the downbeat, we took off. From the periphery of my eye, I caught a glimpse of the alto sax man nodding his approval. He wailed his part then referred back to me for the ending.

The crowd went wild, as did the musicians. "Hey, Phil. She **is** better than you!"

Everyone on the bandstand howled, with Yurtz laughing the hardest. "You got that right," he agreed whole-heartedly as he always did.

"What'a ya say, lovely lady. How 'bout another tune?" the sax guy requested with the rest of the musicians urging me to comply.

"Okay," I volunteered. "How about *Tenderly?*"

At the conclusion of the number, I made my way back to the table where Mom sat at the edge of her seat beaming with excitement and offering a hug. When the set was over, Yurtz joined us at our table and could hardly contain himself, grinning from ear to ear. "Do you know who you just played with?"

Yurtz's grin enlarged to encompass his entire face as I shook my head no. "The sax men are the great Santucci brothers – Jimmy, on B Flat tenor, played with Benny Goodman and Jimmy Dorsey – Nick, on E Flat alto played with Skitch Henderson, Woody Herman, Buddy Rich, and Jimmy Dorsey! **And you gave them directions!**"

Had Yurtz been a silverback and Mom a peacock, their unbridled elations would have been unleashed in their uncontained excitement; Yurtz pounding a pumped-up chest – Mom spreading a glorious plumage. The entire animal kingdom could not have been as proud of their offspring as my parents were for their baby chick at that very moment.

No matter where or with whom I played, my fondest, most special memories were of the performances with Yurtz beside me on the bandstand and Mom in the audience sharing the joy. Yurtz, Mom, and I were a tightly knit trio dependent on each other in all facets of our lives. Where ever I played as a young person – Glen Island Casino, The Mount Vernon Armory, The Bronx Winter Gardens, The Post Lodge, New Rochelle Country Club, Purchase Country Club, Pioneer Country Club, The Davenport Shore Club, among the many – and where ever I still play at the ripe old age of sixty-four, it was and still is in actuality the three of us performing together. Well passed sixth grade, this girl is still actively playing my original horn. Mother did know best after all.

26

Lightning Strikes Twice

The late night club dates were proving to be problematic. Early one Sunday morning, Yurtz, with trumpet case in hand, tripped up the stairs, wavered across the apartment sill, and would have fallen face down on the kitchen floor had it not been for the wall directly ahead of him preventing his descent. Temporarily upright, he rotated along the barrier to his right one hundred and eighty degrees. Hugging the wall, he slid a few feet to his left and grasped at the bathroom door. Accidentally turning the knob, the support door swiftly swung inward catapulting the unsteady body that was leaning against it and holding on for dear life. Yurtz lurched forward, collided full force with the bathtub, and landed belly down in the abyss. Although infuriated by the hour and the inebriate that lay before her, Mom feared for the deadening thump that reverberated as the body slammed into the pit.

Once certain that Yurtz was still breathing as he lay there, Mom delivered the ultimatum. "Once is one time too many," she reprimanded. "If you EVER come home drunk again, I will throw you out of this house for good."

There was no doubt that Mom's tolerance level for such behavior was zero, especially since Yurtz was the one responsible for the safety of the toddler come Monday. To insure he understood even in a stupor,

Mom immediately called for back-up ..... Pop. Within minutes, even at such as ungodly hour, Pop was at the apartment. He entered the bathroom, and unlike the manner in which Mom approached the man in the tub, Pop slowly entered and quietly closed the door behind him. Soft-spoken and calm, Pop worked his will on Yurtz. No matter the situation, Pop was Yurtz's deliverant.

There was an eerie silence in the room for what seemed to Mom to be an inordinate amount of time. Yurtz never revealed to anyone what his father had said, but the impact of that communication lasted forever. It was the first and definitely the last time Yurtz would come home intoxicated, and he rarely, but for only a special day or occasion, imbibe with a cordial of Anisette.

After several years as a school crossing guard earning sixty dollars a week before taxes, Yurtz was hired as a security guard at S. Klein's Department store on Central Avenue in Yonkers. With his non-violent, non-aggressive, non-pistol carrying orientation, he was not a guard in the true sense of the word or duty. Hardly the intended deterrent to two-bit criminals, Yurtz's good nature was better suited to the role of *the greeter* cracking jokes with the workers as well as the clientele.

But between the hellos and the one-liners, the jokester played second fiddle to the musician whose thoughts created melodies on a continuum. Any variant physical location in this world could in no way interfere with his mental location in another galaxy. Like one having an out of body experience, Yurtz's mind functioned as a separate entity on another plane enabling him to view and to hear in dimensions far surpassing the comprehension of average humanoids. He may have temporarily stood at the entrance of the store, but he remained affixed at the threshold of another planet – entering his other realm at will – paper in hand. With actual music sheets unavailable even in a department store housing a multitude of items, Yurtz scribbled music staffs then notes on any available scraps including the backs of punch cards, brown lunch bags, torn receipts, and scads of various reams. There was not a piece of paper anywhere immune from the dabbling dilettante, and melodies were produced on a minute to minute daily basis.

Tending to the business of a routine day, an emergency call from the shop manager summoned Yurtz from his post at the door. A sudden torrent threatened the passive afternoon. The clouds exploded in violent bursts of water flooding the area; the wind whipped forcefully howling at anyone in its path. Yurtz was ordered to close and to secure the chain link fence surrounding the open-air garden behind the facility. The sky was on fire. Covered up in his plastic, hooded jacket and hoping to remain relatively dry under his modest protection, Yurtz ran for his life. With his outstretched right arm, he grabbed one gate pulling it towards him. He repeated the motion until the second gate closed the gap. The sky lit up again. But the mission was yet to be completed. With his right hand, Yurtz reached for the lock which dangled helplessly from the gate, as his left arm dangled likewise by his side. At that very instant Zeus threw another bolt which propelled Yurtz like a B-52 Bomber. His torso slammed the pavement full force rendering him motionless. From the protection of the building, onlookers held their collective breaths at what they had witnessed. A group of co-workers raced to what had been assumed was a corpse and were they themselves shocked to find their friend still alive. Yurtz was immediately rushed to the store's full-time nurse who tended to him before the medics arrived. Dazed, bruised, and yet ever stubborn, Yurtz flatly refused to be taken to the hospital for further analysis. He was driven home.

A knock at our 3A apartment door in the early afternoon was a rarity. Three vertical flights of stairs deterred all door to door salesmen and Avon ladies alike. Mom was preparing Saturday dinner, I was finishing a school project, and Yurtz was at work as far as we knew. We looked at each other with that suspicious *who could that be glare,* neither one of us prompted to open the door to the possibility of a stranger. The faint knock came again.

Well protected behind the locked door, I inquired cautiously. "Who is it?"

A faint yet familiar voiced whined, "It's me, Bobbi."

"Yurtz?" I questioned knowing full well it was his voice. "Is that you, Yurtz?"

"Yes, it's me, Bobbi. Let me in."

Quicker than a flash of lightning, I opened the door. Yurtz stood there making no attempt to come in. Holding his right arm up, I noticed his hand shaking. "Yurtz! What's wrong?"

Mom threw her spatula down on top of the stove and rushed to the door. "What's the matter?"

Yurtz remained motionless, except for his hand which was shaking uncontrollably.

I had been so focused on Yurtz's outstretched arm jerking back and forth that I had not noticed he was crying. Mom must have noticed at the same instant. "Oh, my God! What happened?"

We simultaneously put our arms around him and pulled him into the safety of the apartment. He sat at the kitchen table sobbing for over three-quarters of an hour unable to re-live the horror of his afternoon.

"Tell us what happened. What's the problem? Do you want to go to the hospital?"

Yurtz shook his head *no* as he invariably did whenever hospital or doctor was mentioned.

"Then talk to us!" With still no response, Mom picked up the phone.

"No!" he begged. "Don't call the doctor. Give me a few more minutes."

The coffee in Yurtz's mug trickled out from the rim as his hand motion remained unsteady. He described the incident with vague recollection, the minute details of which escaped his memory bank – unconsciously, he claimed – purposefully, we believed. None of us was ever certain if he had been struck directly with that bolt of lightening or if the bolt first hit the gate then ricocheted off the metal hitting him indirectly. Either way, it was so traumatic an event that he out-right refused to discuss it any further – then – not the following day – not the next week – not ever.

Although Yurtz wanted nothing more to do with that dreaded afternoon, he suffered the mental and physical effects of it for the remainder of his life. Still a young man of some forty plus years at the time of the incident, it was difficult for him to accept the consequences of the aftermath of that horrific episode. Somehow his equilibrium had been tampered with. Once the man so adept at the activities that required fine-tuned balance – playing basketball at the Boys Club, running the beaches of Virginia Beach every morning before sunrise, climbing up and down the vertical steps at 105 one handedly carting a baby and her carriage, and dancing like the great Tommy Tunes of Broadway – now pummeled him. Even the simple, everyday task of walking became increasingly more difficult with age. Suddenly and without warning, Yurtz's body would go askew veering him in directions he had not intended to move in. Though he had not had a drink since Grandpa "Toot-Toot" quietly read him the riot act the night he fell into the bathtub, he nonetheless appeared to be intoxicated as though attempting to navigate his way through an elaborate labyrinth. Mysteriously off-kilter, he stumbled backwards then sideways, progressed forward for a few steps, then stumbled backwards again. Three steps forward – five steps backwards. Although prone to comedic antics, this was not one of them. The first time it occurred, he laughed it off. We laughed with him until we noticed that it happened at unexpected times and occurred more often. This was a matter for medical review not for laughter, but his steadfast stubbornness regarding doctor visits prevailed. Snickering and making light of what Mom and me perceived as a health concern, he diagnosed as a harmless affliction, arguing the only annoyance being, "it'll just take me longer to get where I'm going!" Having neither amused nor convinced either one of us, he quickly added, "Besides – where am I going anyway?"

The back peddling phenomena progressed to a dangerous level. Unable to hold his balance in check, he fell several times that I was witness to and countless times witnessed by others. He hit his head on the pavement in the most unlikely of places – walking from the backyard lot where he had parked the car to the front door at 114 – at Atlantic City while walking from one casino to another – at Gene's dad's house climbing up only two steps to the porch. From then on, stairs, even just two of them, were too difficult for him to maneuver. Worried for his safety, Gene or I walked or stood behind him ready to stabilize him should it have been necessary to hinder a fall. Years and numerous falls later, he had to be rushed to the Hunterdon Medical Center emergency room when he fell and hit his head on the edge of the bathroom sink. "There's nothing wrong with my head," he protested kicking and screaming on the way. "It's still attached!"

Known to countless friends as *The Nose*, Yurtz's prominent facial feature was the brunt of many a joke, the majority of which he told. "I was born in a black out," he quipped. "The doctor pulled me out by the nose and said – it's a boy!" While lying in the emergency room after the fall where he had hit his head on the sink, he alluded to one of this favorite jokes then added, "When I hit my nose – then I'll worry!"

27

Life's Little Lessons

Both of my parents were ahead of their times with their views on humanity. Good people were good people no matter their color, race, or religion, and injustices towards any group were not tolerated in our household. Appalled by the lack of respect given to humankind, my parents, under-dogs in their own right, were in the corner of the unfortunate, mistreated, and maligned in the fight for justice for all, especially when it involved the Blacks and the Native Americans.

I distinctly recall one afternoon at 105 when we were visited by a friend Mom had invited for lunch. During the lively conversation, Mom asked her guest what she would prefer to drink with lunch. The woman indicated she would have a can of soda. As Mom handed her a glass, the woman waved her hand back and forth in the gestured refusal to take the glass. "Oh. That's okay. I'll drink out of the can."

Mom waved right back with her *don't be silly* motion. "Soda is too gassy in the can. It upsets my stomach when I drink out of the can. Besides, it tastes better in a regular glass."

"Really, it's okay," the response was immediate. "I don't want to use your glass."

Mom quickly checked the rim of the glass attempting to decipher the flaw that must have been there. "Is there something wrong with this glass?"

"No, there's nothing wrong with the glass, but if I use it, you may have to throw it out."

Mom winced puzzled by her friend's comment. "Why would I do that?"

The friend offered no verbal response. Her *haven't you noticed* demeanor took a while to click in with the both of us. Our hearts hit the floor. Did this lovely lady at our kitchen table really think that because a black person used the glass we would have to discard it?

Mom immediately removed the can from the table, poured the soda into the glass, and threw the can in the trash. With the liquid in its rightful container, Mom cleared any misgivings. "In this house, we throw the cans away, not friendships."

With that, all was right in our little corner of the world. We had a grand rest of the afternoon, and I had a lesson I would not soon forget.

The day Dr. Martin Luther King was assassinated, we were driving through the South Side of Mount Vernon, the area known, at that time, as the black side of town. Up ahead lining the streets there appeared to be the entire population of the neighborhood – all openly suffering. With headlights shining, two cars filled with the sorrowful passed by us prompting Yurtz to switch on the headlights of our car. "Yurtz," I questioned. "Why are you putting on your headlights?"

The response was in his nature and not at all surprising to me. "Out of respect for Dr. King and the people who love this good man."

By the time we reached the next corner, the light there turned red bringing us to a full stop. Immediately our car was surrounded by a crowd of grievers. Yurtz bowed his head to a gentleman looking in our side window, and the gentleman responded likewise. The light turned green, and although a path was parted to allow us a passageway, our car sat stationary. The light turned red, then green, then red again. We remained. It was when Yurtz finally lifted his head that I noticed the tears. Genuinely touched by the tragedy of this horrific event and by the mourners weeping by the side of our car, Yurtz, who had felt pain many times in his lifetime, felt theirs as well. We finally drove off, headlights on the rest of the way home.

Mom was a devout Catholic never missing a Sunday mass or an opportunity to pray at church or at home with her rosary in hand. Not the church-going type, Yurtz practiced in his own way; by being "a good person." Their means may have differed but the end result was the same. They encompassed others with compassion, respect, loyalty, generosity, and love.

28

I Can Never Go Home Again

It was spring break 1966. The rest of the college kids were departing for distant places in anticipation of a week's worth of unsupervised pleasures far from the rigid rules of life on campus. *They are so misguided*, I thought as I boarded the bus that would take me from upstate New York to Central Avenue in Yonkers. I was antsy the entire way anxious to get home to good old One – OH - Five Spaghetti Drive.

Finally arriving at my stop after the six hour jaunt from Oswego, I leapt off the bus to find Aunt Nancy waiting to pick me up. "Where are Mom and Yurtz?" I inquired. Aunt Nancy explained that the two were busy at home and had asked her to retrieve me. Satisfied with that and totally oblivious to what was really waiting for me at the apartment, I chatted the entire way about the semester that was nearing completion.

When we arrived at 105, it was quickly apparent that something was amiss. The street in front of our apartment was lined with cars belonging to relatives, and conspicuously protruding from the bed of Uncle Danny's truck was my mother's dresser, mirror, and bed frame. Bewildered, I blurted nervously, "What's going on?"

"Oh," Aunt Nancy disclosed. "You're moving today!"

"What? Nobody told me!" I protested angrily as I flung open the front door and darted up the first flight of stairs. *This cannot be happening.*

As I stomped up the second flight, I nearly knocked over Uncle Danny and Uncle Charlie who were coming down the staircase fighting to keep the weighty wrought-iron kitchen table from slipping out of their grip. "What are you doing? Where are you going with my table?" I kept demanding answers but received none that I wanted to hear.

"You're moving. Hurry up stairs. You can help carry your clothes down."

As I attempted to process what was happening, my bedroom dresser scraped passed me pressing me into the wall. "Stop! Take that back up," I yelled to no avail as the dresser then the cedar closet pushed past.

I stormed up the third set of steps reminiscent of the day my mother stormed up when my dad had left me alone to go gambling. By the time I reached the top step, I was already beyond panic stage. Aunt Anna was standing at her door, and I could tell by her downtrodden look, this situation was for real. I ran towards her outstretched arms, and as another piece of memorabilia left for parts unknown, we both started to cry, taking refuge in each other's grasp.

No one had informed me about a move. It reminded me of the year prior when Yurtz's mother, Grandma "Toot-Toot" died. I did not find out about that critical day until I came home from college thereby missing the chance to say good-bye. I felt like screaming, and had I not been encompassed in Aunt Anna's arms, I probably would have.

"How can you do this to me? Where are you going?" I challenged my parents who were stepping into the hallway ready to descend with yet another piece of my past. "Why didn't you tell me before this?"

"We have to move now. Aunt Jo and Uncle Al are moving out of 114 Valentine Street today, and we are moving in there. The arrangement happened so fast we didn't have a chance to let you know."

That explanation was not good enough. Any explanation would not have sufficed. This situation was totally unacceptable – like Grandma "Toot-Toot's" death being kept from me. All of this was unforgivable, and I let my parents know it in no uncertain terms.

I removed myself from the clutches of Aunt Anna and fled into my apartment for the last time. Making my way through the five rooms, I stopped then sat on the floor in each room to mentally relive the fond memories that, like my tears, came flooding forth.

As is the case for the majority of Italian families, the main gathering area for our family was the kitchen. It was the hub of my education, and more important than just the place to complete school work, it was a never-ending learning center. There were the thousands of hours of the essentials of music both in the observation of the brilliant master at work and in the participation of each facet of that which was created. I was the genius' sounding board; my opinion sought from the titles of the pieces to the keys to the rhythms to the orchestrations. The truth of the matter was that, although appreciative of the welcomed opportunity to add my two cents into the pot of a quad-zillion dollars, it was never necessary for me to either ante up or edit that which was perfect and way beyond my scope of musical knowledge. Nonetheless, I was gratified and loved the inclusion into Yurtz's world of thought. And in that other world, it was Yurtz in that very same kitchen who taught me the dance steps to the polka, rumba, waltz, tango, Charleston, cha-cha, and the lindy as we shuffled about on our own private linoleum dance floor three stories above the street.

The kitchen was also the hotbed of cookery, as I learned the fine art of Italian cuisine – Mom style – as well as the art of macaroni variation – Yurtz style. The game of how many meatballs can be stolen from Mom's gravy took place every Sunday. Mom had a count of every one of those delectable rounds and knew the minute one was missing. If Yurtz had taken one, she would explode. But if I confessed to the crime of pillaging, the threat of eruption fizzled. I became Yurtz's front man in the quest for gravy laddened orbs, and although we howled at the thought of putting one over on Mom, she knew who the real culprit was all along. In addition to the usual unexpected Sunday guests who seemed to drop in at just the right time to join us for lunch, our diner played host to many a weary performer.

Our living room was the hub of noise making. There were countless hours of trumpet practices in the closet and sessions with Uncle Mike and Vinny. Michelle, Vinny's younger sister and later to be my Goddaughter, astonished us as a dancing vortex, spinning for hours to the music being played. How she remained steady on her feet was a mystery to the rest of us who were dizzy just watching the whirligig.

On the weekends, we gathered around the fifteen inch, black and white television that was our focal point. Sunday mornings were especially riotous as we roared through the antics and misadventures of Chaplin, Laurel and Hardy, the Marx Brothers, Burns and Allen, Jack Benny, Abbot and Costello, Amos and Andy, and the Keystone Cops. In the afternoons, Uncle Charlie contributed to our ear piercing screams as we cheered for superstars Paul Hornung then Bart Starr and the rest of the Green Bay Packers.

Our rebel rousing continued as we rooted for the Native Americans to rally victorious against the old West cowboys and the government agents and military men that annihilated them on screen and in real life. The spirit of the underdog lived within us, though our trials could in no way compare to the atrocities they suffered. We took them in as part of our family and held their culture in as high a regard as we held our own.

My parents' bedroom was my doll house as I played there every chance I had. One favorite pastime was to scour Mom's dresser drawers to marvel at the costume jewelry sparkling like trillion dollar Tiffany diamonds and emeralds. The truth is that Mom never owned even an engagement ring from Woolworth's much less jewelry requiring the Lloyd's of London insurance. Yet, no matter how often I gawked then removed the fake, precious baubles from their Charlene boxes, their brilliance and beauty, much like my Mother's, never ceased to overwhelm me. With the jewels adorning my every inch, I paraded in my Mother's spike heels and wedding gown, eventually ruining what I had later wished I had been able to wear on my own memorable day. Perhaps that was for the best as I could never have done justice to it as she had.

The day of the move from 105 was as traumatic for me as the day my parents moved from Mount Vernon some twenty-eight years later. Where were **my** things? As an only child I took ownership of all that existed in **my** world at 105, all property being **my** personal property. The objects being removed from **my** world were **my** dressers, **my** jewelry boxes, **my** gown, **my** one and only childhood doll, Maria, **my** chair – the one I sat in with my legs draped over the arm rest while writing my deepest thoughts in stories and poems. And most importantly, where was **my** favorite item – the Lucchine dog house?

Hanging on the kitchen wall to the left of the dumbwaiter was a hand-made wooden plaque which had rested there from the time I was born. The plaque was adorned with the front entrance of a three-dimensional dog house aptly etched, *Lucchine Doghouse*. Along side of the house and to its right sat three wooden cut-out dogs. Although each canine was easily distinguishable by size, our names, *Phil, Mary*, and *Bobbi*, were engraved to ensure further proper identification. When any one of the three of us did something the other two were not enthralled with, the pet with the corresponding culprit's name was placed on the hook inside the doghouse. As I recall, Yurtz was in the doghouse most of the time, but my puppy had its share of time-outs too. So, where was **my** doghouse? In the mad scramble to leave the apartment, a source of pleasure for over twenty years had vanished and was never to be located again.

I readily admit to being selfish, but, then again, I felt entitled and compelled to hold on to all that I cherished. At that moment, without advanced warning and time to grieve, all that I had known was being ripped from me, hauled down the staircase, one item after another. As I sat on the floor sobbing, I knew I could never reveal the real truth for my abnormal attachment to our apartment. A life-altering situation occurred years prior, and this home was my safe haven.

The actual year of the occurrence had been buried with my sanity and so deeply concealed in the crevasses of my mind that it could only be retrieved more than fifty years later through the counseling I should have received as a child. Nonetheless, the event itself never escaped me. A male adult molested me. The fondling occurred one other time, and to keep it from ever reoccurring, I kept my distance from the perpetrator as much as physically possible.

Photographs of me between the fourth and fifth grades show an abnormal weight increase during that time. Weight would become a life long battle, as I inflated to a one hundred-fifty pound fifth grader. By sixth grade I was well on my way to obesity, tipping the scale at one hundred-sixty pounds. Eating and playing the trumpet were the two avenues allowing me escape routes from my inner demons. I was obsessed by both. By the time I was first chair trumpet in high school I was breaking the dials at one hundred eighty-five pounds. No wonder the boys had difficulty accepting me at first. How dare a girl – *a fat girl* – play better? I was ballooning to dangerous proportions, and inhibition and self-conscientiousness dominated and stifled my every move. Subsequently even one of my escape routes, performing on stage, became a nightmare as I was forced to stand in front of those assessing not only my playing, but, more so, my size. I hated myself.

During my senior year of high school, I literally starved myself in order to shed forty-five pounds hoping for a date to the prom. That never happened – but the yo-yo dieting did, continuing throughout adulthood. As a freshman at college, I felt the need to loose as much weight as possible. I boiled one dozen eggs and ate a one or two eggs meal a day. This regiment lasted for four days, stopping only when I passed out on campus walking from one class to another. My secret was eating me alive – yet I confided in no one.

I was resolute to maintain a normal outward appearance, a performance for which I could have been awarded an Oscar. My room and my home at 105 became my sanctuary, the only place I felt free from the danger that lurked in the outside world. I often hibernated refusing to leave the house even when urged to go out and enjoy life. But I could not fully enjoy any aspect of teenage life wondering who might touch me or where it might happen again. I was safe in my domain and spent hours writing poetry. At the time I was not quite certain of the meaning of my written words. Now those words scream their intent:

> On a surface serene my ship sails,
> Yet deep within the chaos prevails.
> All afire, my inner soul melts,
> A betraying loneliness is felt.
> From afloat one may say,
> The sea does quiet, calmly lay.
> But the truth escapes the passerby.
> Can't see or hear the one who cries.
> Out of control I'm damned to spin,
> Until I'm rescued from the hell within.

The lonelier and more alienated I became, the more I retreated unto myself. I turned to those comforts I knew best – eating any sweets I could get my hands on and playing my horn, which I know saved me from further self-destruction. Through it all, I became self-sufficient and dependent only on myself, realizing I was the only person I could fully trust. As a teen and young adult, I surmised that if I remained obese, I would be safe from unwanted advances. I stayed clear of aggressive men.

I was enraged and distraught at having to deal with the wretch who stole my childhood, my dreams, my relationships, my self-esteem, and my ability to function normally or as what I perceived as normal in others. The aggressor was free to live undetected and unpunished, while I was caged in with the profound burdens of guilt, sadness, loneliness, weight issues, self-conscientiousness, resentment, and a deep depression that had to be covered up with a happy façade lest the unthinkable be discovered.

My bitterness, fury, irritability, and temper increased with the passing years, and it was not until the death of my beloved lifesavers, my parents, that I finally sought help from that which tormented me every day of my life. And, it was not until it was too late that I came to the disturbing realization that, for all those years, I had taken out my frustration, depression, and anger on my Mother for reasons yet unexplainable. For as much insight and intuition as she possessed, she still was not a mind reader.

Had Uncle Charlie known, he would have killed the rat-bastard; a term he used to describe any low life he despised and loathed. Had Mom or Yurtz known the torment their perfect little girl endured, it would have killed them both. My parents were my security blanket, my saviors, the ones who loved me unconditionally, and yet I could not divulge this to either for fear of causing their deaths through heart-break. Although I should never have felt guilty for something that was clearly not my fault, the tonnage of that pressure stifled my every move and every thought. I missed out on the many pleasures of life as a child, a teen, a young adult, and an older adult as well. Even my Lucchine, God-given talent was wasted. The pleasantries and the *what could have been* in my life can never be recouped, and for those reasons, the perpetrator can never be forgiven.

Had my parents known how much the apartment at 105 meant to my sanity, I am certain they would never have opted to move from Mount Vernon Avenue. As I sat, fanny on the tile and back propped up against the bedroom wall, the questions kept coming: *Why move now? Why move at all? Would I be safe? What was so special about 114 Valentine Street?* Yes, it was only one of three small, brick apartment buildings on a quiet, tree-lined street of quaint, one family homes. The neighborhood was certainly a serene setting far from the truck traffic of Mount Vernon Avenue. And yes, the location was a convenient one block walk to the hospital, City Hall, and the police station with an additional two blocks to the downtown shopping area on Fourth Avenue. But 105 was just as convenient as far as I was concerned. Questions racked my brain. *What aromas would we inhale ascending the stairs in an apartment only partially occupied by Italians? How could I get along without seeing Augie, the little Italian grocery store owner beneath us, who had become like a grandfather? And how could we ever survive without sharing our everyday lives with our across the hall family – Uncle Mike, Aunt Anna, Vinny, and Goddaughter Michelle?*

To some, the move my have seemed like a step up from where we had been, but that did not matter, especially to me. One – OH – Five Spaghetti Drive was my home, the only home I had known for twenty-two years. My safety net was being torn apart with each piece of furniture careening down the staircase almost as fast and as out of control as my heart. I was confused, upset, angry, and hysterical.

With the apartment cleaned out, everyone was ready to leave but me. I still had much to think about and to process. Through my tears I saw the figure of Aunt Anna before me. Her shy smile and demeanor akin to Princess Diana's always brightened my day. But this day could not have been any cloudier. She assured that our families would forever be one, as a few blocks separation could never come between us. As she continued to console me with her memories of our past twenty-two years together, my tears subsided with each happy story.

"Remember when your parents bought their very first car in 1954?"

"Of course," I smiled. "It was a Chevy Bel-Air in red and white, Mom's favorite color combo," I replied with fondness in the memory. My euphoria was fleeting as I made eye contact with the red and white tiles on the floor and sunk back into the doldrums.

"As I remember," Aunt Anna offered quickly to lift me from the depths, "your mother insisted that she had to have a car no matter what the cost."

"Well, everyone she knew had a car, so why shouldn't she? After all, she was thirty-five years old and Yurtz was thirty-seven. Neither one had ever driven a car let alone owned one."

"The problem was," Aunt Anna reminded, "that neither she nor your dad even had a license yet!"

"Yeah," I acknowledged as I wiped away the last tear rolling from my reddened eyes. "How crazy was that? We finally had a car but couldn't even use it. Every Sunday," I chuckled, "we'd go downstairs, sit in the car that was parked in the street all week long, have a snack, and then come back upstairs."

"Well at least they didn't have to buy gas," Aunt Anna laughed.

"Can't argue with that. They certainly saved a ton of money there," I affirmed giggling. "But after a couple of weeks of sitting in a parked car, my mother was aggravated that we still weren't getting anywhere!"

I was okay with that. I may not have been going anywhere in reality, but I went everywhere in my imagination. Mom was more bent on reality. "That's when her determination kicked in, and she obtained her license. Yurtz was shamed into getting his license a few weeks after that."

"Do you remember the first place you drove to?" Aunt Anna inquired hoping to occupy me with happy thoughts.

"How could I forget? We went on our first family day trip up to what we called *the country*. Back then, we considered any area with a few trees – *the country*. Grandpa Curto owned six lots in Lake Carmel, New York, and believe it or not, he bicycled there from Mount Vernon. He'd peddle those fifty miles on his dilapidated bike, hang out awhile, and then peddle fifty miles back in time for dinner. I don't know how he managed that."

"Me neither," Aunt Anna commented shaking her head in disbelief. "I can imagine how grateful he must have been to be finally driven there."

"Grandpa Curto was not the only one excited at the ride to *the country*. I was beside myself the entire trip and could not wait to lounge at the mansion by the lake. Boy was I shocked when we arrived. We turned off the main road, headed uphill for several blocks, and made a right turn onto a dirt road. After passing several two-room bungalows in dire need of renovations, we pulled over to the side of the road."

"We're here!" Mom announced joyously.

"We're where?" I questioned in bewilderment.

"We're here at Grandpa's!"

Where's the mansion? I asked myself as I scanned the area. All I saw was a dirt road and a lot full of trees, weeds, and boulders. The terrain descended sharply in all directions and was littered with ruts as deep as the Grand Canyon. We attempted to walk into the woods, but the lopsided ground caused too many missteps that could have easily fostered a tumble. There wasn't even a run-down bungalow much less a mansion. We removed our folding chairs from the trunk of the car, lined them up along the dirt road, and ate macaroni in front of our car facing the lot. After an hour we loaded the car and drove back home. We could just as easily stayed home and had lunch in our car in front of the apartment! But Mom was overjoyed, and that is all that really mattered."

Aunt Anna and I had a field day with that story, and I know she kept reminiscing about the good times to keep me from breaking down again.

"Remember the time you ran away from home?" Aunt Anna questioned knowing full-well that I could never have forgotten such an episode.

"I could never forget that day," I smiled remembering the day as though it had happened the day before.

Like many children, I crossed the fine line between acceptable and not acceptable behavior a few times in my childhood landing me in the doghouse. Although *the look* was all that was ever needed to keep me on the straight and narrow, it was inevitable that I would test the boundaries. In one of my feisty, stubborn, five-year old moods, I had a disagreement with my parents, the gist of which being unimportant compared to my father's rein on me. "If you don't like it here," he remarked with a semblance of what he himself had been told in shop class, "you can leave!"

With that ultimatum, I removed my dancewear and my tap and ballet shoes from their valise and refilled the suitcase with a few items necessary for survival away from home. Packed, I headed down the stairs, out the front door, and stood on the corner of Mount Vernon Avenue and High Street, a few doors away from the door to our building. As I stood there contemplating my next move, I was unaware that both of my parents were watching over me, heads protruding from the third floor window.

Mom, agitated by the outcome of our confrontation, expressed remorse and grave concern seeing her little girl alone on the corner. "Are you sure she's okay out there by herself? What if something happens? We won't be able to get down there fast enough."

Quietly Yurtz watched as Mom continued nudging him to do something. "The cars and trucks won't stop. How can you be so sure she will be okay?"

"Trust me, Mary. I know my daughter. She always obeys me."

"Obeys you? You are not the one in danger. Our daughter is on that corner alone and in possible danger."

"Danger? She's not in any danger," Yurtz assured. "I'm telling you, she'll be just fine. Wait and see," Yurtz asserted with certainty.

Mom, not comforted by those promises, kept her eagle eyes glued to the street and her baby. As the clock ticked, so did Mom. She had had enough. Over an hour had passed and no one was making a move towards resolution. "Go get her now or I will," she demanded.

"I don't have to," Yurtz affirmed what he had known all along. "Here she comes!" Yurtz gloated as both watched me heading into the hallway.

"What makes you so sure of yourself?" Mom questioned as she sighed with relief knowing her daughter was climbing up the stairs.

Can't remind Mary of the incident three years ago when I left Bobbi on the chair alone for hours to find her still sitting there when I returned, he figured. *Guess I never have to remind her – she has never forgiven me for that.* "You'll see," Yurtz responded with an air of smugness.

The knock at the door signaled my arrival.

"Who is it?"

"It's me, Yurtz."

"Who's me?" Yurtz turned to Mom and giggled softly so as not to give himself away.

Quite annoyed at his shenanigans, Mom reprimanded, "Will you open that door – now."

"It's me, Bobbi"

The door opened. Yurtz stood blocking the entrance. "Well, what is it?" Mom bit her lip and grimaced with that *come on already* look.

"Can I come back home, daddy?"

"Well, just a little while ago you were running away from here. What happened?"

Looking up with tears in my hazel eyes, I submitted, "You told me I can never cross the street by myself."

"Yes, I did say that, didn't I," he repeated to insure Mom understood his power. "Well, I guess in that case, you can come back home."

Yurtz turned to Mom nodding with that *I told you so* demeanor as I stepped safely inside the apartment and into my room. That night after hugs and kisses from the two people I loved most, I was tucked into my comfy bed. And as I laid my head on my fluffy pillow and curled up snuggly under the blankets, I knew in an instant that Dorothy was right all along – *There's no place like home.* And for me, there would never be another home like *One – OH – Five Spaghetti Drive.*

29

Blow By Blow

When spring break began I could not wait to get home, but merely a week later, I was anxious to get back to the familiar surroundings of the sorority house. For the remainder of my years in Mount Vernon, 114 Valentine Street would never feel like home to me.

At first Mom loved her new place, which was a stone's throw from both of her sisters, Nancy and Julie. Although he never stated so, I believe Yurtz would have preferred to have remained where he had been, but the one facet of the move he truly loved was the closeness of his two sisters-in-law he adored.

One Sunday morning while Mom was in church, Yurtz walked the two blocks from the apartment on Valentine Street to Aunt Julie's house on North 7th Avenue. The front door locked, he trekked down the driveway, climbed the back stairs, and knocked at the door.

"Anybody home?"

While waiting for a response, he was surprised to find the back door unlocked. He stepped into the foyer and followed his nose to the source of the tomato and garlic aromas. There on the counter next to the stove was an above ground, pool size tub of macaroni overflowing with meatballs and smothered in Italian gravy. The aromatic scents and accompanying visuals were too tempting to resist. *Don't mind if I do* he thought as he wolfed down his second helping. Mass completed, the family returned home to find their Sunday meal a quarter of the size it had been. But all knew better than to report a burglary. "Uncle Philly was here!"

Other than that situation I could not understand what was so special about the new place. We still had to climb three flights of stairs, granted they were not vertical as there were landings mid-way up each flight. There was one less room, and with the same lack of closet space, it was even more difficult to store items. The kitchen was half the size. I was thankful Yurtz taught me to dance in the kitchen at 105, as there was no room to maneuver fancy footwork in the mini space at 114. There was a dumb-waiter that had not been used in years, and because it had been permanently sealed, the daily chat with neighbors was non-existent. With four separate apartments on each floor rather than two, the probability of a close-knit extended family feeling had vanished. Of the twelve families, we only knew three, and those were simply to greet and make small talk with. The only family we had a close connection to was in the next door apartment, mainly because they were dear friends of Uncle Al and Aunt Jo and we had known them before we moved in. I missed my grocery store grandfather, Augie, Aunt Anna, Uncle Mike, Vinny, and Michelle. I even missed Eleanor's melodious summonses, "Eeeeeeeent......aaaaaaahh......kneeeeeee!"

I longed for the comradery of the musicians who once hung out at our place. The only intermittent visitor was my Godfather, Uncle Tommy, whose blindness was the main factor he could not come over more often. With less than tunnel vision and diagnosed legally blind, he had no choice but to rely on others to drive him to and from our house, which Yurtz did often. I always ran downstairs to meet him at the front door then escorted him up to our apartment.

Reliving old times, Mom, Yurtz, and Uncle Tommy created the stuff of legends. We gabbed. We laughed. We gabbed. We laughed. And then I cried. The simple pleasure of eating had become a major challenge for my beloved Godfather as utensils were indistinguishable and had to be selected for him – then handed to him. Uncle Tommy, the once steady-handed Gene Krupa of the Vernon Troubadours and the Palmer Orchestra, whose sticks never missed a snare or a cymbal, missed the bowl of meatballs on the table. Subsequently, we made certain the bowls of whatever the fare was for the day were directly beneath Uncle Tommy enabling him to eat the only way he was able to – by lowering his head literally into the bowl. And I cried every time. Suffering with the debilitating, continuous progression of sight loss, Uncle Tommy's visits became less frequent. We kept in constant contact by phone, and I looked forward to our weekly conversations, as Uncle Tommy's spirit always uplifted mine. "How's my Ba Ba Lu?"

Life was more difficult and at times dangerous at 114. Although the neighborhood may have looked superficially safer, it was not totally what it appeared to be. At one point, a heroin addict resided with his mother in one of the apartments. He was well known by all the tenants, and though he had yet to pose a threat, everyone treaded cautiously throughout the building. When the four rather expensive wire rim hubcaps were stolen from my new 1969 Mustang, my mother confronted the habituate about the theft, and although she had the notion he had stolen the goods, she requested his aid in finding what had been swiped. Miraculously, the wheel covers were returned two days later.

Stolen items from a car were not life threatening, but an apartment break-in could have been. With the exception of the dim light from the living room television, my parents' apartment was dark and seemingly unoccupied. Alarmed at a strange noise coming from the kitchen, they proceeded cautiously to investigate. There on the fire escape directly outside the kitchen window was the shadow of someone attempting to gain entrance to the house. Having pried open the window, the perpetrator's head leaned forward beyond the plane of where the exterior meets the interior. As he rested one foot on the sink inside the apartment, the hardened user was coiled to spring forward the rest of the way into the kitchen.

Grabbing the longest knife she could find in a hurry, Mom ran towards the window howling like a were-wolf. "What the hell are you doing here?" she screamed as she threatened the intruder with the thick, sharp blade wheeling crazily in a zigzag motion in his direction. Mom was an expert at slicing meat, and his meat was as good as dead meat if he ventured any further.

Startled by the outburst of a convulsive Zorro attacking from what had been surmised as an empty apartment, the addicted one yanked his head and foot out of the apartment falling backwards onto the metal grates. "Oh. I thought I was climbing through my mother's window."

"Like hell you thought that," Mom challenged with the implement still flailing wildly. "Your apartment is on the other side of the building. You were here intentionally. If you ever, ever, ever come near here again, I'll............" But before she could complete her threat, he was gone.

As far as I can recall, the incident was not reported to the police as the boy's mother begged forgiveness, and my mother felt pity for the poor woman. Mom rationalized that he did return the hubcaps, which he admittedly had stolen, but nonetheless, this would be his final straw, making it perfectly clear that if he ever came near our family again, she would have him arrested. That week, the window was fitted with a full-length iron gate, which locked from the inside of the kitchen and further insured the safety of the family. Or did it? The lock was virtually impossible to open once secured, and had a fire broken out, the escape route would have been sealed. It was definitely not the safest of situations either way.

Mom, in pain most of the time from her back injury, found a new job at the sprinkler factory on McQuestion Parkway. She either had not been fully informed of the dangers of working with acid or she honestly did not realize how very dangerous it was. That coupled with the lack of proper sized protective gloves became her worst nightmare. The gloves, which fit only to the wrist, had a fold-over cuff that accidentally collected the caustic she was handling. When reaching up for a needed item, the corrosive liquid poured from the cuff onto her arms, then seeped inside the glove penetrating the flesh of her fingers.

Teaching in New Jersey at that time, I was unaware of the accident, but when I made my routine call home as I did with the frequency of dusk, the conversation did not sit well with me. Mom was not available to speak, and when Yurtz indicated that everything was fine, I could tell by his voice that it was anything but. That Friday I headed home for a surprise weekend visit, but Mom and Yurtz were not nearly as surprised to see me as I was surprised at what awaited. Shocked to see Mom's both hands and arms up to the elbows bandaged with gauze, I was horrified to learn of the accident that had left her severely charred with the right side in worst condition. The first time I removed the gauze for treatment, I felt nauseous at the sight of her burnt flesh. In the healing process of soaking then gently salving the wounds, the pain was excruciating, and as brave as I always knew Mom to be, this was too unbearable to pretend otherwise. Recovery was a brutal, torturous process for all of us as we felt her pain though not in the magnitude she felt. I took a week off from work as did Yurtz, and we monitored and tended to the dressings continuously throughout that hellish week. It took months before Mom could put the worst of this ordeal behind her.

Not long after that Mom's eldest brother, Uncle Frankie, passed away causing her more agony than the acid etching of both arms. Her entire body system fell prey to the shock of this profound loss and triggered the onset of diabetes. Mom was inconsolable. She had endured the relentless, oppressive burden of daily survival for her entire life, and this normally vibrant, illuminating soul collapsed into a deep state of depression. Referring to her condition as a *nervous breakdown*, she left for some much needed mental and physical rest with friends in Florida.

With her revitalization, Mom returned to her former self only to have additional setbacks. After hospitalization for a hysterectomy and eight weeks of recuperation, she once again needed surgery.

Years prior, Mrs. Glenn, a weekly customer at the Grand Union in Pelham Manor, had befriended my mother even to the extent of inviting Mom and me to be her guests at the country club she belonged to. When learning of my mother's eminent surgery, Mrs. Glenn enlisted the expertise of her husband. Dr. Glenn, Head of the surgical unit at the New York Hospital, performed the foot bone surgery himself.

While in her own painful recovery, Mom became the pillar of strength for her hospital roommate. Rose Ann Waltz was facing a complicated surgery with the prospect of blindness as an outcome. Before then after the surgery, Mom and Rose Ann, who Mom nicknamed *little soldier*, prayed together hand in hand.

"I will never forget Mary," Rose Ann wrote. "As sick as she was and in all the pain she was suffering with her feet, she would get up during the night when she heard me crying and bring me water and hold my hand. She told me not to give up, to keep fighting, and to have courage. I always loved her for her goodness. I consider myself lucky to have been a part of her life. Mary, never forget how much I love you."

Keenly aware of the financial situation of our family, the surgery and the hospital stay were compliments of both Dr. and Mrs. Glenn. Overwhelmed by the magnanimous generosity of the Glenn's, Mom cried for days. With her deepest, heart-felt gratitude, Mom thanked the two every chance she could with cards, notes, and letters filled with "love and prayers." But that alone could never have been enough to satisfy Mom. Because the Glenn's refused to accept payment, Mom mulled over alternative ways to thank the pair. Having owned *fine china* from Woolworth's Five and Ten Cent store, Mom relished the thought of finally being able to select a tableware pattern formal and exquisite enough to be placed on the table of the Head of State not to mention on the table of the Head of the Hospital. Mom meticulously scrutinized then selected the most elegant Lenox China tableware, but as per usual, her taste far exceeded her pocketbook. Fortunately, with the pattern she opted for in open stock, she was able to purchase one or two settings at a time which she hand-delivered to their home on consecutive Christmases until the set of twelve had been completed. They loved her for it.

With our lives returned to normalcy, life pressed on at 114. The three of us adjusted to our new environment at our own speeds. My adjustment, being the slowest, finally led to my resignation that the move was permanent. I resigned but never conceded further to the new address. Whenever I visited later on in life, I was going to visit my parents – not going home.

30

It's All In The Head

No matter the residence, be it 105 or 114, the kitchen table therein was invariably cluttered and piled mid-way to the ceiling with music manuscripts. In this seemingly chaotic conglomeration of music paper, score sheets, note pads, and any other forms of paper that Yurtz could use to scribble his musical thoughts, there was order – an order only he could decipher – but an order nonetheless. He knew the location of every scrap of paper and what had been written there. Along side the heaps rested two inkwells - one filled with blue fluid - the other filled with black fluid. Pens with various size nibs lay in front of the wells waiting to be submerged.

Yurtz worked best well before sunrise or well after sunset when Mom and I would be asleep. He required uninterrupted, dead silence and an all-consuming focus when creating charts for bands. Not only a composer of original music, he also scored music from Big Band to Jazz Band to Swing Band to Society Dance Band to Dixieland Bands to Marches to Classical Orchestras --- for all instruments – in treble or bass clef – in any key – in any rhythm – in any style. When called upon to orchestrate by the leader of a particular group, Yurtz invariably asked these questions – *What song? What key? How many men? When do you need it?* At the moment the phone disconnected, the arrangement was as good as completed in his mind-set. To study Yurtz's lengthy process enabled me to gain insight into the mind, heart, and soul of an anointed one.

Yurtz accompanied his vocalizations of each instrumental part by air playing the instrument he was writing for. To witness the orchestration proceedings was truly an amazing, mind-boggling experience. Observations of his hand and finger motions divulged the instrument he was mentally playing.

Naturally, the trumpet was represented with three fingers mimicking the valves he pressed as each note blared forth while fingers gliding horizontally along the table top represented the piano ivories being played. With his thumb gently touching his index and middle fingers, Yurtz slid his hand vertically from his mouth to his waist in the creation of the trombone part. While cupping his hand and strumming horizontally, he played the upright bass. When all fingers were in motion, the positioning of his hand divulged different instruments. A hand held vertically from the mouth signaled the clarinets, but when the hand was held at the side of his body, the saxophones blew their part. The drums incorporated foot tapping along with a thumb up tight fist motioning as though hitting the snare or the cymbal.

Brief pauses between measures allowed Yurtz the time necessary to transfer the notes he had just created from his psyche onto paper. The arrangements came alive on music sheets one note at a time, as he dipped his special pens in the inkwells with the transference of each note. There was a particular size pen for notes – another for symbols – and yet another for terms. Add to this – a color code; black for music notes, blue or black for written words, and red encircled the key signature and the tempo. Like the grand master, Michelangelo, painting murals on chapel walls, ceilings, and canvasses, Yurtz painted his masterpieces on five-line staffs with his delicate, hieroglyphic symbols scripted with perfection and carefully positioned on or between the lines as he willed. Note by note, the pain-staking manual process to complete one full band arrangement required days or even weeks, dependent upon the particular type of arrangement requested.

How can anyone be so conscientious at five o'clock on a Sunday morning, I contemplated while still half asleep. Totally unaware of my presence, Yurtz continued tapping his foot in rhythm while maneuvering his fingers as though pressing the valves on his trumpet. I stood there engrossed in his every move as I always did when watching him create music. Catching a glimpse of my shadow over his shoulder, Yurtz greeted my presence. "Hey, sleepy head. Come join me," he coaxed as he quickly cleared a small area of the table large enough for two cups of coffee.

"What are you writing?" I inquired as I sat down and took a sip of caffeine strong enough to keep me up for the next two days.

"I wrote a swing number for the Post Lodge band. Two more sax parts and it'll be ready to blow. We'll try it out next weekend." With that, Yurtz seemed to pass into one of the trances I was use to witnessing during his creative process. The spells lasted varying time periods depending on his mood and intensity of thought. I quietly continued to sip my drink knowing he would eventually snap out of it.

"Hey," he startled himself back to Earth. "How's this for a title? *Rockin' At The Post.*"

"Great name," I acknowledged.

"Yeah, man. That's it. *Rockin' At The Post.* It's a Basie number if I ever wrote one!" he boasted proudly not knowing then that his words would someday be validated. "The guys'll flip!"

The guys always flipped over Yurtz's songs and arrangements. Conductors and band directors from the tri-state area commissioned his services, and although his time, energy, technical ability, and genius should have been heavily compensated for, he usually wrote for gratis, especially for friends.

After one particular concert band performed an original composition, one of a very few musicians Yurtz did not know from a different musician's local group curiously questioned him. "What method do you use to write and arrange all the parts?"

Yurtz shrugged his shoulders at the reference to *a method*. *What is a method?* he confessed to himself that he had no idea what the musician wanted to know.

"Guys went to college to learn to arrange," Saul recently confirmed what we had known all along. To a college-groomed musician, the question was perfectly logical. To Yurtz, the musically uneducated, the question came from left field and made no sense.

"Yeah," the guy pried again. "I'd like to know which method you use."

Yurtz clued the guy in with the only response possible. "I use the Lucchine method!"

"Who's Lucchine? A professor somewhere?" Baffled, as though his music theory course had omitted an important minute detail in his education, he pressed for more information. "I never heard of Lucchine or his method."

"I'm Lucchine," Yurtz pointed out with that *are you kidding me* attitude. "I'm Lucchine."

"You're Lucchine? So, what is your method?"

"It's all in my head, man!" Yurtz responded in earnest trying to explain his method. "I hear every note for every instrument and write each part out as I go along."

"Do you play the chords on the piano?"

"Piano? I don't own a piano. Like I said, I hear the chords in my head then write them down. It's all in my head."

The gentleman's forehead wrinkled in an attempt to comprehend a method totally foreign in the world of the musically educated and certainly far beyond what would be expected from a high school dropout.

Yurtz belonged to three musicians unions: Local 402 of Yonkers, Local 802 of New York City, and Local 38 of Westchester County where he was elected to and served on the Executive Board. In 1970, of the 980 members listed in the Local 38 directory, only 8, including Yurtz, were designated arrangers, less than one percent of that total population. Although both areas increased in 1980 – 1131 musicians with 12 listed as arrangers, the percent of arrangers rose very slightly to a mere one point one. A drop occurred in 1991. Of the 1092 musicians, 10 met the category of arranger, again dropping the percentage of arrangers to less than one. Further declines were noted in 1997. Out of the 709 musicians listed in the Local 38 directory, only 5 were listed as arrangers – a mere point seven percent. These statistics document the high degree of difficulty, specialization, and rare talent required for this skill. Arrangers are an infinitesimal, elite microcosm of the entire realm of musicians.

Yurtz felt strongly that arranger were the most "under-appreciated" and "under-rated" of the musicians. I was most fortunate to have his expert analysis of every piece of music we ever listened to. "Do you hear the key change? Listen to the accented beats in the next measure. Do you hear the trombones countermelody? What do you hear now? Listen to the syncopation in the next set of measures. Did you hear the rhythm change? Is the key the same? What instrument is playing? How about the change-up?" The questions were endless, the learning process intense, and the dissection of every measure was pointed out verbally or vocally or with hand gestures. To this day, when I hear music, it is the arrangement that captures my attention.

No matter the genre, the arrangers are the backbone and the life of each piece. It is their placement of notes, the intricacies of rhythms, the blending of chords, and the instrumentation thereof which make the music what it is, an elaborate assemblage of sounds prompting responses from tears to joy. Yurtz was the master of this musical world, and all who knew him in that realm, were, as I, in awe of his incredible genius.

31

The Buts Have It

In the early 1950's Bill McCune headed south and continued his career in Miami Beach, Florida. With the dispersion of the McCune group, Yurtz played on weekends with various musicians. He headed for New York City and landed a steady weekend gig at the Hotel Edison. Ironically, having experienced failure at one Edison during his youth, he found success at another Edison in adulthood playing there for several years.

While in the City, Yurtz knocked on many publishing house doors only to have his music deemed unsuitable for the new rock era sweeping the nations teens off their feet and in the process, smothering the big band era of the teens of the recent past. "Your music is great," publishers acknowledged. "**But** it's not what we're looking for." Yurtz once told the Daily Argus Newspaper, "you get a couple of those knock-downs and you say forget it."

Although the Big Band Era was slowly fading away, Yurtz was determined to keep his music alive. Using his original charts, he created his own twist on the forties genre, a Big Band composed not of professional roadmen but of the most talented neighborhood teenagers he could summon. And when the piper called, the teens showed up with instruments ready. The trumpet section consisted of three of

Yurtz's top students and featured Noah as the premier player. Gifted teen Anthony Maise, whose father, Tony, played with Yurtz on many club dates, led the saxophone section. To round out the ensemble there were trombonists, a drummer, and, of course my *brother*, Vinny DeGloria, who later became widely known as Vinny Dee. Without a doubt, Vinny Dee, who would later play professionally with the Riff Nordone Trio, was the "greatest young genius" on guitar. Riff referred to Vinny "as his left arm on background guitar. His chords and keen ear for different sounds made him a bundle of talent in a still very young man. He is the best chord man in the business."

Practices were held weekly at Saint Mary's Church Hall on the corner of Mount Vernon Avenue and High Street. Not only was the facility perfect in size and location, it was, more importantly, rent free; a huge factor for the leader housing an empty wallet. With the joints jumping everywhere the band performed, the group was much sought after for local dances at Saint Mary's Hall, the Westchester Woman's Club, and various local venues. The boys jumped at the chance to enter a band competition that was being sponsored in the area. The only Big Band entered seemed to be overshadowed though not out-played by the hordes of rock bands that had entered the competition as well. After several rounds of elimination, the top two groups stood awaiting their fate. The judges preempted their decision by pointing out that the Big Band was outstanding, "**but** it's not today's music." It was the term **but** that indicated the final result. The runner-up position would not have been so devastating had the winning group had half the talent.

Teaming up on several compositions, Yurtz's music and his sister Rose Reisman's lyrics blended beautifully for the ballads and love songs they created together. After years of rejection, the pair thought they had finally found the Rosetta Stone they had been looking for. As it turned out, the big break they needed was in Aunt Rose's backyard all along.

Aunt Rose's dance and vocal studio in the Bronx, New York spawned notable performers thereby allowing her contact to record producers. Nurturing a young prodigy named Gennaro Vitaliano was her crowning glory. At her studio's annual recital at the Bronx Winter Gardens and then at the Westchester Woman's Club, the handsome, boyish-looking singer, whom Aunt Rose ordained as Jerry Vale, mesmerized then captured the hearts of every woman in the audience. Taking center stage amid the ballet dancers, their pink feathered fans surrounding him, Jerry Vale became the headliner at each annual revue.

With his popularity reaching far beyond the boundaries of the Bronx and Mount Vernon, Jerry Vale, the newest recording star, stood by the piano in Aunt Rose's living room and crooned the Lucchine-Reisman masterpiece, *One Night One Rendezvous*. With Jerry's magnificently pure intonations, the duo's signature work took on a life of its own. We cried. He vocalized again. We cried again and every time he delivered his euphonic sounds.

One evening, Jerry drove us home in his white Cadillac. By that time, our car was a dilapidated rust heap that had holes in the floor boards in the front seating area. Yurtz joked that we could have used our feet dangling through the openings as either an extra set of brakes or as a way to start the car in motion. It was no wonder that Mom was enthralled as was I not merely by being chauffer-driven by a famous recording artist but, more so, for riding in such a luxurious set of wheels. Not only was the floor solid beneath our feet, the seats moved up and down and back and forth with the push of a button.

"Someday, Mary," Jerry predicted, "You will have a car like this one too." That was music to Mom's ears as she floated up the stairs believing that her husband was about to *hit it big.*

There would be many magical evenings in Aunt Rose's living room listening to Jerry and the music duo collaborating together. Never had any of us ever imagined the depth of the meaning of that song until Jerry poured his heart and purity of voice into it. There was no doubt that *One Night One Rendezvous* was to be a smash hit as Jerry had promised to record it. **But** that never happened. The singer took off for glory, never looking back or keeping his promises. He left those that helped him launch his career permanently docked on the pad.

Through Aunt Rose's connections, Yurtz was given the opportunity to be the musical advisor of a new variety show that was to be televised. Aunt Rose, Mom, and I accompanied Yurtz to the home of the pre-selected piano player whereupon the informal audition commenced. We sat quietly through their discussions and musical interludes, and it became quickly evident that their musical styles, forethoughts, and personalities meshed harmoniously. The project demanded the collaboration of similar mind-sets, which for them gelled instantaneously. It was indicated right then and there that Yurtz would be the man for the job. Beside himself and ecstatic at the prospect of the opportunity to infiltrate the frontier he so desperately sought to conquer, Yurtz was ready to set sail. **But** his ship never left port. Word came that the network did not pick up the show, leaving Yurtz to sink once again.

In 1975, Yurtz entered America's International Songwriting Competition sponsored by The American Song Festival of Hollywood, California. Thousands of songs poured in from all over the country as well as the world, and we anxiously awaited the results. The evaluation read, "We are pleased to inform you that your song had made it to the second level of screening. This accomplishment means that your song was in the upper seven percent of all ASF entries and was evaluated by at least four screeners. We are unable to provide you with further information, **but** we hope that this will encourage you in your songwriting efforts."

On several occasions, Saul commented then lamented, "musically, Philly was way ahead of his time.......**But** he just never got a break."

Yurtz indicated numerous times that he wished he had had a dime for all the **BUTS** in his life. "I would have been a millionaire."

32

Rockin' At The Post

The Music Maker Is Floatin'

There were no *buts* within Yurtz's circle of musician friends where the story was different. Yurtz was revered and highly respected for his incredible talent, being recruited for his trumpeting as well as his compositional arrangements.

He landed a permanent weekend gig at Glen Island Casino, the *Home of The Big Bands*, in New Rochelle, New York. Although the term casino evokes thoughts of gambling in today's mind-set, back in the 1920's through the 1970's, Glen Island Casino could not have been further from that scene. Cozy offshoots of the Casino hosted weddings and gala parties while the grand ballroom provided live entertainment and dinner and dancing in a swanky nightclub atmosphere. Many of the most famous top groups of the Big Band Era performed in the main room including the ever popular Glen Miller Orchestra. The original owner, Angelo Bartolotto, was so overwhelmed to have booked this extraordinary orchestra that he actually carried the signed contract in his pocket to show any and all who would be impressed by that. At the time, Glen Miller sported an eighteen-piece band and was paid five hundred-fifty dollars for the entire group and the evening's entertainment. The one staple among the various bands and live shows that changed weekly was the **Nick Marra Band**. Considered the Casino house band, Yurtz played with and orchestrated for the group for well over ten years.

One evening at Glen Island, Bill Schuback, bandleader at the Pioneer Country Club in the Catskills, directed a show at the Casino. When he heard Yurtz and Bill Fafley playing the horns, he was blown away. For a musician playing a one-time show with typically fifteen minutes to review his part, a phenomenal sight-reader is a must. And both men were just that.

"I could really use one of you guys," Schuback offered. "The job entails a steady six nights a week. Friday is the Jewish Sabbath and rest day. Which one of you guys can I count on?"

Bill Fafley flatly refused the offer – Yurtz accepted it.

The Pioneer Country Club booked high profile talent including singers Toni Arden, Billy Eckstein, and Billy Daniels and comedians Totie Fields, Jackie Mason, Jack Carter, Henny Youngman, Pat Henry, and Pat Cooper among the notables. The shows were elaborate extravaganzas, and Yurtz loved being part of the magic of such talented people.

For two years, Mom and I suffered through Yurtz's absence. He came home every Friday by noon, leaving all too quickly Saturday by three. A vital portion of our trio was missing all week, and all of us were lonely. Mom and I visited the Pioneer several times and were fortunate to have been granted special privileges while there. We stayed with Yurtz at the musician's house on the grounds of the Country Club and were allowed to dine, free of charge, with him in the main dining hall. The tree covered hills provided a serene setting, free from the hustle and bustle of the truck traffic on treeless Mount Vernon Avenue. For us, it was a vacation in the country and one we could never have afforded had it not been for the generosity of the club owners who wanted to keep my dad happy for as long as possible. They needed him – but we needed him more.

The grounds of the country club included a magnificent golf course which provided Yurtz with his own entertainment during the day. While overseeing the course, the club's golf professional noticed Yurtz having difficulty swinging the clubs. After discovering the problem was a paralysis of the left arm, the pro taught Yurtz a grip and swing method that would allow him to play. Having been a pretty decent athlete at one time – a basketball wonder at the Boys Club as well as a faithful runner on the Virginia beaches – Yurtz honed his golf skills. From nine to one and from two to four daily, Yurtz was on the course. Yurtz actually surprised himself when on a the par thirty-six nine hole course, he scored a thirty-seven.

One quiet morning at the course, Yurtz was paired with comedian Jackie Mason's brother. Excited about his one over par the previous day and feeling confident he could make par this day, he swung with all he had. As luck would have it, he missed the shot completely, and though not a foul-mouth man, he blurted out, "Oh shit." As he and his partner walked to the next hole, they passed several people strolling the path next to the course. Tipping their hats, they greeted Yurtz's partner, "Good morning, Rabbi!" Yurtz would have sunken into the hole had it been large enough to contain his body. He began to sweat profusely and offered an immediate apology. Mortified and embarrassed, he was quite surprised at the Rabbi's reaction as he laughed all the way to the final hole.

Two years of one-nighters at home took its toll on all of us. Yurtz returned home with a new sense of appreciation for those he had left behind, a situation akin to that of the weeks he left Mom in Nebraska while he was in Indiana with the Blue Barron group. After this second experience, he would never again take the jobs that had him on the road away from home, and for the remainder of his playing days, he traveled within the Tri-State area.

After the Catskills, Yurtz's main gig was as a principal with the **Post Lodge Band** in Mamaroneck, New York. Along with fellow Vernon Troubadour and Joel Palmer original Joe Tanno on bass, the group rocked with Frank Fraioli on piano, Tony DiSantis on Drums, Mike Piazza on trombone, and occasionally trumpeter Bernie Privin, who was a regular with the Ed Sullivan and Jackie Gleason show bands. Added in to the mix were the extraordinary talents of the illustrious Santucci brothers, saxophonists who blew with the likes of the Dorsey Bands, Skitch Henderson, Buddy Rich, Benny Goodman, and Woody Herman. With this assemblage of elite musicians, the rafters jolted on every number.

During shows, Yurtz gained favor among the comedians; several offered to take him on tour – not as a trumpeter but as a plant in the audience. With his contagious belly laugh, he would insure the response intended and make the comedians look good. As tempting as those offers may have been, he continued his stint with the trumpet.

For over ten years, Yurtz soared with the "guys that were out of this world." His original Basie type composition, *Rockin' At The Post*, became the Lodge's theme song, and each week when the guys blew the house down wailing their theme, *The Post was definitely Rockin'*.

After the Post, Yurtz played one-night club dates with a variety of groups, some with various leaders and other where he was contracted as leader. As diverse as the occasions, the clubs were equally so. He played gigs from the New York Athletic Club to the Westchester County Center to area colleges to every New Rochelle shore club in existence at the time.

A favorite haunt became the Good Times Room at Yonkers Raceway, which, on more than one occasion, proved to be quite a challenge for the boys in the band. Between sets and sometimes between numbers, the guys slipped me money to place bets on their favorite equines. Even Yurtz got in on the action, and although the point of the gig was to line the pockets of the musicians, the propensity towards favorable tune selections did not carry over to horse selections. The lack of winning tickets made for an expensive evening, and the gig quickly became a non-profit proposition for all, as each man went home with less than what he had started with.

Yurtz was hired to join a "pick-up band" at County Center in White Plains, New York. It was "a bunch of guys on a club date," but for Yurtz, this night was to become anything but the usual club date with friends. In addition to the scheduled show, the Center was hosting a surprise guest that even the instrumentalists were not cued in on.

Prior to his arrival on stage, Mr. Jimmy Durante, famed and much beloved singer and comedian known for his conspicuous olfactory and bandstand antics, surveyed the guys in the band from his backstage vantage point.

"Is there a guy in the band with a big nose and a good sense of humor?" Durante inquired.

The response was immediate. "How 'bout Phil Keen, the trumpet player?" the show organizer suggested.

"Yeah. I spotted that trumpet player right away," Durante confessed as to what he had noticed. "He's got the nose all right. But can he take a joke?"

"No question about it," the organizer affirmed.

This statement was verified that evening and again fifteen years later in an article featured in the Daily Argus newspaper, which described Yurtz as "an easy-going guy with a big nose, unpolished diction, and an untamed sense of humor that would never pass in swanky clubs." The paper reported what his friends had known for over sixty years, so it was no wonder that he had been affectionately selected as Durante's target for the evening.

"He's a funny guy who can tell a joke a minute himself," the organizer added with confidence.

"Okay, then," Durante committed. "He's my man!"

The band continued the show tunes with Yurtz so focused on sight-reading his music he was unaware of what was brewing behind the scenes. The crowd went wild at the sight of the comic legend, *The Great Schnozzola,* Jimmy Durante taking the stage, exuberantly waving his characteristic hat and flashing that irresistible ear to ear grin that overwhelmed even his most prominent facial feature. Just seeing one of his idols was enough to send Yurtz into a tailspin. Jimmy had not said a word yet and Yurtz was already laughing. Durante's type of guy to be sure.

As the crowd noise died down the band took off with Jimmy's hit, *Won't You Come Home Bill Bailey?* Now seated at the piano, fingers roaming up and down the keys, Jimmy came in with his gravel voice belting the tune. With a few jokes interjected between his first song and then his signature number, *Inka Dinka Doo,* the crowd rose to their feet. While shaking his head and his hat in rhythmic jerking motions, Durante's trademark routine kicked into high gear.

"Stop the music," Durante demanded signaling the silence of the instrumentalists. "Stop the music. Stop the music!"

By now the world knew what that meant, and people were already laughing with anticipation. Slapping his hand on the top of the piano, Jimmy stood up. "I can't believe it," he told the audience then pointed to the back of the bandstand. "Look at the nose on that trumpet player!"

Before Yurtz could catch his breath from his last note, Jimmy picked up the sheet music that had been sitting on the piano and whipped it towards the *other nose* who was now hysterical.

Not skipping a beat, Durante continued, "Just look at that nose! That trumpet player is trying to steal my job!"

As Yurtz looked up in time to see more sheet music whipping past his head, he heard on of the guys warn, "Watch out, man. Here it comes!"

Another set of sheet music flew tangentially past Yurtz's nose, and just when he thought the assault was over, a piece of the piano whizzed by Yurtz's head as he quickly ducked from the flying wooden object. The piano was ripped apart one piece at a time, each segment flung towards Jimmy's big schnozzola rival on the trumpet. Everyone roared – none harder than Yurtz whose entire being exploded with laughter then gasped for air for the next surge of hysteria. With his breath completely out of control, Yurtz may have need resuscitation had the show not restarted when it did. Durante's set continued without the trumpet player who laughed through the finale.

Perhaps their meeting was in the cards all along, as there seemed to be an uncanny connection between the two men right from the start. Both men were born in New York and in the month of February. Each quit school and opted for lives on the road as jazz musicians – Jimmy on piano – Yurtz on trumpet. The two men were master comedians with "unrefined diction" and tremendous senses of humor. Neither man ever made fun of nor teased the shortcomings or physical features of others. Jokes were directed at themselves. Each had an only child – a daughter. Jimmy worked tirelessly to raise money for handicapped or disabled children – Yurtz was himself a handicapped, disabled child. Whatever the conjuncture, Yurtz held Jimmy in highest esteem and was his greatest fan. When Jimmy became ill, Yurtz and Mom sent Jimmy letters, notes, and cards filled with jokes, love, and prayers. Upon his death in 1980, Jimmy's wife sent Yurtz and Mom the prayer card from his viewing, a treasured memento to thank two special fans for their friendship and well wishes through the difficult times.

In August 1970, the **Charlie Miles Band** with half of the **Post Lodge** group including the great Santucci boys, Frank Fraioli, and Yurtz merged to form a gargantuan ensemble. Charlie elected to play Yurtz's original swing numbers – *Floatin', The Singing Trumpet, Good Time Blues, and Rockin' At The Post* – to an audience of 1200 music lovers at Mount Vernon City Hall Plaza. The joint was definitely *Floatin'*, but Yurtz would float highest at the Hilton Hotel.

One evening at the Hilton Hotel in New York City, two guest musicians, who had been with the original Count Basie Orchestra, joined the Charlie Miles mega-band for a one-time show. Once again Yurtz's big band original pieces and arrangements were featured. Upon the completion of the orchestrations, *Floatin', Good Time Blues, and Rockin' At The Post*, both Basie men simultaneously turned around to acknowledge Yurtz who sat at the back of the bandstand. Offering their public critique, both men smiled their approval. With their thumbs-up gesture and the yes head nodding, they summed up their evaluation, "Yeah, man! You nailed it! Yeah, man!"

Yurtz nodded and smiled back, and although he appeared superficially cool and collected, he was anything but. Without a wing on him, he could have flown into outer space. In fact, he never really came down from his high, and on more than one occasion proclaimed that **this single event was the one that "MADE MY CAREER!"**

33

The Music Marches On

The virtuoso's mind never ceased to create. While viewing a movie or a show on television, Yurtz often times deadened the sound and vocalized his own soundtrack to compliment and set the tone of the action on the screen. His improvisational music was mind-boggling, as he changed the vamp scene by scene and show to show in an instant.

In 1965, former gifted trumpet student, Bob Nelson, called from his dorm room at Lehigh University attempting to persuade Yurtz to write a special version of *The Carnival Of Venice* for the *guts squad,* a trio of trumpeters who needed a challenge for their up coming concert. "None of the versions we've played are up to speed," Bob explained. "Our conductor wants to showcase our talent, but we can't seem to find a trio suitable."

I recall my father's part of the conversation. "Sorry, Bob. I don't think I can do it. I've never written any classical music, and I don't want to leave you boys up in the air."

The voice on the other end of the line continued pleading his case, knowing he was speaking to the most gifted musician he had ever known.

"But, Bob," Yurtz pointed out again. "I'm a jazz – big band writer. Classical is not my thing." Although the phone conversation ended with friendly good-byes, both men were nonetheless disappointed at the outcome.

I was in total shock having never once heard Yurtz decline to create an arrangement. When I inquired what Bob had requested and Yurtz revealed what had transpired, I immediately stepped in. "Well, why don't you at least try to write something?"

"But I don't write classical music," Yurtz retorted trying to convince both of us.

"It doesn't hurt to at least try – does it?" I shrugged as I planted the seed in his creative head.

Musically, I was certain that Yurtz could do it all. And for him, a seed of inspiration planted and a confidence booster was all he needed, as the following day he scribbled out his first version of the trio. After sending the preliminary score to the University music professor for a test toot, the search was over. It was just what the Doctor ordered! Yurtz received the full band score so he could refine and incorporate his trumpet trio version into the background arrangement. When asked his fee for the work provided, Yurtz simply said, "This one's for Bob." The thank you letter from the University professor with a tape of the trio playing during the May 15, 1965 concert was all that was required to make him a happy man. Payment in gratitude and in the enjoyment of sharing his talent and his music made Yurtz happiest, and that evening we celebrated his classical success with a toast, a glass of wine, and a feast of macaroni and meatballs fit for Niccolo Paganini himself. What could be better?

With that venture completed, Yurtz delved into another new music realm and produced his first march. A marching band consists of a more varied instrumentation than a swing band. The orchestrations for oboes, bassoons, tubas, French horn, flutes, piccolos, and bass clarinets were new challenges, but Yurtz tackled them with the same intensity, his perseverance paying off with the completion of the full arrangement. In August of 1967, *Marchers Delight* premiered at the Mount Vernon Municipal Band concert. The summer series program under the direction of Doc Randall was a weekly event and one the entire town looked forward to. The City Hall plaza, which was packed with music lovers, was a perfect setting for concert goers. Yurtz's march was hailed as a huge success by both Doc and the crowd who showed their approval with an eruption of applause in a standing ovation. All of us there to support Yurtz were overwhelmed as Doc called Yurtz up to the stage to acknowledge him further. From then on in Doc and Yurtz had a deep respect and admiration for the other's talents, and music would be the bond in their dear, lifelong friendship.

One of the greatest feats in human history moved us to tears. For days, we were glued to the live broadcast of the 1969 three-man Apollo mission to the moon. As the lunar module touched down on the moon's surface for the first time ever since the creation of the universe, the astronauts signaled their safe arrival. "Tranquility Base Here. The Eagle Has Landed!" The drama unfolded before millions around the world, yet our emotions were so closely tied to the event, we felt as though we were there with the men on the moon and taking part in their heroics ourselves.

I awoke the next morning to find Yurtz at the kitchen table, pens in hand, sheet music cluttering the surface. "I couldn't sleep last night," he divulged. "I kept hearing the astronaut's words and a melody that wouldn't quit."

"Is it a swing number?" I questioned knowing quite well that it always was.

"No." he smiled. "It's a march."

"A march?" I could not believe the jazz master before me had a second march hidden in the depths of his cranium. My curiosity was piqued.

"Yeah. It just came to me, and I couldn't get it out of my mind. I even can't believe I just wrote another march. I'm naming it, *The Eagle Has Landed*, in honor of and in dedication to the astronauts."

"Wow. How fabulous is that? Sing it for me, Yurtz."

I listened intently as Yurtz tapped his foot to the drum beat and pealed the rejoicing melody in a brisk tempo. During the second stanza I chimed in to the rather catchy tune, as Yurtz would want anyone listening to do the same. "Simple is better," he often said. "I try to make it as simple as possible so people can understand the music. It's more enjoyable when people are able to sing or to hum the tune easily."

And his new march certainly had that body swaying, euphonic element. "It's great. I love it. What a terrific tribute," I shouted then hummed again.

"Now all I have to do is to write out all the parts," Yurtz decided with my enthusiastic response.

The Eagle Has Landed premiered in December of 1969. Performed by the Port Chester, New York High School marching band, who had been selected to participate in the Rose Parade. The march was an instant hit, as its melodic counterpoint could have rivaled any march ever composed. In honor of his brothers, Pat and Henry, who served in the Navy during the War and to commemorate the feat of the Apollo astronauts, Yurtz sent the march to the United States Navy Band in Washington, D.C. The response came from Commander D.W. Stauffer. "I have placed your number, *The Eagle Has Landed,* in our new music book for trying some time in the future. It will be evaluated for our possible use." With that note, Yurtz landed on Mars!

The Eagle landed on Doc's desk, and in August of 1971, the Mount Vernon Municipal Band played the march at City Hall. Popular with the musicians as well as the crowd, word traveled, and again the march was featured a month later at the Labor Day concert in Untermyer Park in Yonkers, New York.

In 1972, I accepted a teaching position at Hillsborough High School in central New Jersey. Because it was a newly incorporated school of three years, many aspects of the school still needed attention. With the lack of a school fight song and me as the cheerleading coach, I commandeered Yurtz to remedy the situation. The school's original fight song, *Raiders On The March*, debuted in the November 1973 pep rally. Yurtz and Mom accompanied me to one of the football games. That day Hillsborough handled its opponent 28-0; the band played the new fight song as the cheerleaders and the crowd accompanied with vocals. The Daily Argus newspaper reported, "that may not have been as dazzling as a gold record, but it meant just as much to Lucchine." When asked how it made him feel to hear his march after every touchdown, he confessed, "I was crying a little bit." That year the football team rallied to an undefeated season, and some conjectured, "it's gotta be the song!"

Doc played whatever Yurtz wrote, and in August 1977, he conducted the Municipal Band in the *Senior Citizens Of America March*. This was exciting for all of us, but especially for me having the distinct honor to write the lyrics to another one of my father's pieces. As the band marched on, the crowd sang joyously honoring the senior citizens of our country. Doc loved the march so much he played it twice in a row and then again at the conclusion of the evening.

In 1980, The Daily Argus newspaper, which serviced Mount Vernon and the Bronx, sponsored a march contest open to residents in the vast distribution area. Rather than name identifications, the entrants were to place the first three numbers of their social security identities on the top of the sheet music to insure a fair assessment of the pieces by the team of judges. The winning entry would be awarded the distinction of forever being known as the Daily Argus March, and to entice further participation, a one hundred dollar stipend would be issued.

There was plenty of interest in the contest – just not enough musicians who could write then arrange the full score. Most average citizens, including those associated with initiating the contest, do not comprehend the magnitude of talent and time required for this massive undertaking. In light of that, two entries were received, one being my dad's. At the August 2nd Municipal Band concert, the two works were performed as the judges tallied their opinions. When the announcement was made, "*The Daily Argus March* is number 062," everyone in our contingent screamed, none louder than me. I erupted, "You won, Yurtz. You won!" as mass hysteria broke loose in our section of the audience.

Jumping up high enough to qualify for the Olympics, Mom screamed proudly, "That's my husband. That's my husband," as the tears came gushing forth.

Yurtz sat quietly for a moment while the chaos continued around him. *I won? I won?*

At the front of the bandstand, Doc called for number 062 to come up to the stage. Still in disbelief, Yurtz had to be pried from his chair. "Get up there, Yurtz. Doc is calling for the winner."

With a shove towards the front, Yurtz made his way through the crowd and on to the platform.

"Hey," Doc exclaimed smiling so radiantly he could have made lead melt. "It's our friend Phil. Our good friend, Phil Lucchine. Come on up, Phil."

Extending his hand, Doc reached out to congratulate Yurtz who could not hold back the tears any longer. Genuinely happy for the winner, Doc embraced Yurtz and whispered, "This is a terrific march, Phil. I love it."

Standing there in tears before the assembled, Yurtz was totally overwhelmed not only by the audience applause and Doc's response but, more importantly, by the fact that he was finally being appreciated by his community as the brilliant composer and arranger that he was.

Before the conclusion of the concert, Doc asked Yurtz to stand up and once again be recognized. "And now," Doc concluded as he singled out a still tearful composer standing in recognition, "we will end this concert with Phil Lucchine's own – *The Daily Argus March*." With that, the band commenced as the citizens of Mount Vernon showed their approval.

The following Monday morning, Yurtz's photograph appeared on the front page of the Daily Argus, and as part of their update of the contest results, the photograph was accompanied by a two-page article about the composer.

The one hundred dollar stipend meant nothing.

The recognition – everything.

34

Decrescendo Allegro

Late 1980's – Early 1990's

I was witness to the heart-wrenching day the universe collapsed in on Yurtz crushing him with debilitating finality. The lip, which had been Yurtz's Achilles' heel since his surgery as a young man, fell prey to the loss of the only teeth left able to hold dentures in place. Without teeth, vital in the support of lips pressing against the mouthpiece, playing a brass instrument is impossible. At the time, Yurtz knew two horn players that had had implants to replace their dentures, and although neither musician friend was ever able to blow after that, Yurtz was desperate to give it a chance. After many disappointing appointments with various dentists, Yurtz accompanied me to a session I scheduled with my dentist.

After the examination, the doctor revealed his grievous assessment. "I'm so sorry. You can certainly have the implants, but, even with those, I'm afraid you will never be able to play the trumpet again."

Yurtz sat in the dental chair and broke down in hysterics. Standing behind him during the examination and the painful outcome, I grabbed a hold of him in what was a vain attempt to provide solace to the inconsolable. The doctor left us to mourn in private.

"I thought I'd be able to play forever," he sobbed in writhing pain. "I thought I'd be able to play forever."

We cried together as we had many times, and in that moment, as other moments had been throughout our lives, his pain was for me just as real as if it were my own. I believed then, as I do now, that I alone, save the true musicians with whom he shared this tragedy, comprehend the magnitude of this profound loss; the depth of which being as suffocating and as debilitating for him as for a former prima ballerina having had limbs amputated or a world-class athlete left a quadriplegic after a neck injury. The suffering incurred by this master trumpeter was incomprehensible, for unlike the dancer or the athlete with their visible disabilities, Yurtz's crippling ordeal was not readily visible to the masses and thereby rendered his pain undetectable and unto himself. The horrifying reality surfaced often and arose in him a sadness that robbed his spirit.

One afternoon while we viewed a television special dedicated to a then ninety-two year old jazz pianist, it became quite evident that fingers, which in younger days would have glided effortlessly over the keys, were noticeably straining at a slower pace. Yurtz glared at the tube as though mesmerized. I thought he was totally engrossed in the music, but I was incorrect. At the conclusion of the program, Yurtz turned towards me, and with tears streaming down his cheeks, simply said, "At least he can still play."

It was neither the music nor the tempo Yurtz honed in on. It was the fingers, though slower and more deliberate, still enabling the pianist to continue to create his music. I have absolutely no doubt that if Yurtz had been given the option of being boiled in oil or not ever being able to play his beloved instrument, he would have opted for the scalding, as the torture inflicted by that pain would pale in comparison to the torment of not being able to blow the horn. Not even the make-shift solutions of playing from the side of his mouth or growing a mustache for bulk or using upwards of ten different mouthpieces like he had done after lip surgery could alleviate the disfigurement this time. He was pummeled by the nightmare he could not awaken from.

For Yurtz, the words, "you will never be able to play the trumpet again," were as excruciatingly agonizing as a mouthful of exposed nerves in dire need of thirty-two root canals. To him, death would have seemed a better option, as the anguish of that day never went away – not for a moment – not for the rest of his life.

When Yurtz lost the ability to play his horn, he also lost the will to compose. "There's nothing new anymore," he would say to me, and as an excuse not to write he added, "I don't have *it* anymore."

The truth of the matter was that Yurtz would always have *it*, but not the *will* to go along with *it*. This was a mental death – and it was final.

The person that he had been would never be fully alive again. Tormented, he withered in to his own quiet inner sanctum.

35

On The Move – Again

Late 1980's

My parents applied for and were offered an apartment in the beautiful, brand new senior citizen's complex across the street from the Mount Vernon police department. Mom was desperate to leave 114 for a variety of reasons. First, but by no means foremost, was the condition of the bathroom ceiling. More than a mere eye-sore, the massive, ever widening hole became a convenient passageway for water to gush into our apartment with each flush in the apartment overhead. At times, mostly inconvenient ones, pieces of corroding ceiling tiles rained down on those using the facility.

The second dilemma involved the interior temperature which could not be regulated on an individual basis. The apartment sweltered in degrees that would have instantaneously melted the world's ice caps, inundating inland seas to the level of the flood waters in our bathroom. The only inhabitants able to survive in this seething condition would have been lizards and water lilies. Contacting the landlord was as fruitless as Death Valley, but contacting Saul was the oasis needed. As a professional plumber after the road days, Saul assessed the situation and literally took the matter into his own hands. He disconnected the radiator then moved it out into the hallway next to the perfectly sized indentation by the door. Non-functioning as a source of thermal energy, the newly positioned radiator served well as a platform upon which the groceries, instruments, reams of musical scores, packages, and various other item could be set when unlocking the door. No more fumbling with keys – no more soaking saunas to contend with.

With that solved, the focus was on the third and certainly the foremost of the quandaries – the escape window in the kitchen offering dubious protection with that damn iron gate. Without the bars, a criminal could enter then escape. With the bars, a criminal could not enter thereby ending the need to escape. On the other hand, once the residents, my parents, entered through the door, they could not easily escape out of the window covered by the locked gate, God forbid, had it been necessary to do so. The solution whether to remove or not to remove the bars was simple – move out. Certainly, I did not help the situation by constantly pointing out that these problems never existed at my precious 105.

As desperate to move as Mom was, she and Yurtz knew there were others in greater need. They waived their right of occupancy in the new senior structure and pleaded to have their apartment given to Aunt Anna and Uncle Mike who were still residing at 105. Aunt Anna had been house bound for years, and at those rare times she did get to leave her confines, she had to be carried down then up those three sets of vertical stairs. For an aging Uncle Mike, having difficulty negotiating the stairs himself, carrying another person down then up was a monumental task equal to climbing Mt. Everest. Impossible. My parents convinced the powers making the tenant selections to grant the elevator equipped housing to their dearest friends.

Shortly after Aunt Anna and Uncle Mike were settled into their new place, my parents left 114 Valentine Street as quickly and as mysteriously as when they had left 105. Before I could finish playing *Rock Around The Clock* on the trumpet they were informing me of their new address in a Third Avenue senior building. Mom sounded happy so I refrained from making judgments until I actually saw the place.

As a privately owned building, it was not government sanctioned as senior housing per say, and none of the amenities provided at a true senior complex was offered. As far as I could gather, the only qualifications necessary for this structure to be labeled senior housing was that all the residents were elderly and the building was as old as the Pleistocene Epoch. I figured this was not a good move but kept my mouth in check. After all, the apartment was in close proximity to Hartley Park and the Armory, where senior activities abound and where Yurtz, who had been employed as a van driver for the seniors at the Armory, knew all who frequented both facilities. Before he lost the ability to play the horn, Yurtz provided the music for the senior dances and was everyone's favorite jokester. Perhaps knowing the complex and the people would be their saving grace.

The public parking lot was only a one block walk to the apartment, yet for a senior citizen carrying groceries, it might as well have been in downtown Manhattan. The lot was dimly lit and invited the threat of trouble for those unsteady on their feet. When visiting my parents one afternoon, my husband, Gene, and I parked in the lot. While walking towards the ramp that led to the street, a full can of soda flew past us from the street below just missing Gene's head by a centimeter. The hoodlum who threw the can fled the scene, leaving us to wonder what might have happened to a senior citizen in his/her rightful place at the wrong time.

The entrance to the apartment was unlocked and unguarded, and the halls, screaming for an uplifting, fresh coat of Sherman Williams, were a drab color last painted when a Neanderthal was hired to do the job. The dreariness was accentuated by the dim lighting. In fact, it was difficult to see beyond one's arm length and begged the troubling questions of *who might be waiting on the elevator or lurking in the hallway.* The ever so clever seniors had those questions covered, and their solution tested at least one time that I am aware of.

One quiet afternoon, there was a knock at my parent's door. Not expecting visitors, Yurtz cautiously peeked out of the eye hole. Standing there was an unfamiliar, ominous figure of a man. Smartly, Yurtz backed away from the door on tip-toes so as not to be heard within the apartment. Silently he motioned to Mom who stepped into the kitchen cubbyhole to call the neighbor next door with the red alert. The knock came again. Yurtz and Mom stood motionless lest they make a sound and be discovered by the unwanted guest waiting by the door. Apparently unwilling to call attention to himself by kicking the door in and creating undo noise and chaos, the hooligan finally moved to the next door. No one answered there either. Hoping for someone to respond by opening the door and inviting trouble in, the perpetrator proceeded down the hallway hitting each door as he passed. But all of the neighbors in that hall had been alerted one by one and stayed clear of their doors. One of the neighbors had the task of calling the police who arrived within minutes. From the safety of their locked apartments, everyone heard the commotion in the hallway. With the volume of a bull horn at its highest decibel, the cops shouted, ordering the hoodlum to drop his gun. This frightening situation did not sit well with me, and I was frantic for my parents' safety from that moment on.

The two and a half room apartment was compact, to describe it at its fullest. It consisted of a bedroom large enough for army bunks. The living/dining area was the combined size of the interior of our '54 Chevy, and there was a bathroom where the use of the commode necessitated painful gymnastics positions. Minuscule to the point of being shockingly more claustrophobic than the closet Yurtz use to practice in at 105, the kitchen left everything to be desired. Standing dead center, one could simultaneously scramble eggs on the stove with the right hand while washing the pans in the sink with the left hand. The Italian feasts and the aromas thereby produced were gone – along with the desire to remain there.

With the kitchen storage space for food and the pots, pans, dishes, and other essentials necessary for food preparation being non-existent, the days of vats of meatballs and gravy and pounds of spaghetti cooking on the stove were over. Perhaps that was for the best as the mice would have had a field day. To say the place was infested with the disgusting little rodents is to make an understatement. Their presence was quite clearly marked with the aftermath of their food binges in the kitchen. Before bedding down on the pull-out couch, Gene and I had to clean up after them. I rarely had a good nights sleep squirming from the possibility of facing one of those rats as I turned over.

As if those problems were not enough to send people into hyperventilation mode, the windows in my parents' apartment suite overlooked what my mother referred to as the Berlin Wall.

The only good thing about the place was that it was in Mount Vernon, my parents' beloved city. But even that was not incentive enough to keep them anchored. Their ship was sailing.

36

You Can Take Them Out
Of Mount Vernon

But You Can't Take
Mount Vernon Out Of Them

1993

A momentous occasion occurred on February 7, 1993. We gathered at Our Lady of Mount Carmel Church in Mount Vernon to celebrate the fifty year anniversary of the marriage of Phil and Mary. It was a happy occasion, though I cried through the entire renewal of vows ritual mass. For one-half of a century my parents had endured life's roller-coaster ride with dignity and resolve. I could not have been prouder nor could I not have been more thankful that God had chosen them to be my parents.

As I watched my heroes approach the altar to receive their blessings, I realized for the first time their physical fragility. Life had taken its toll, and Yurtz, age 76, and Mom, age 73, appeared to me to be older than their years. This frightened me until I recalled my talks with the Father when I was a young girl. Mom told me that He would grant me any wish if I attended a Novena for nine weeks. Every Tuesday evening I walked the half-block up High Street to Saint Mary's Roman Catholic Church and participated in the rituals of the Novena – for the first nine weeks – then the second nine weeks – and every nine week unit after that for all the years we lived at 105. I prayed for my parents. I prayed that they be granted long, healthy lives and for their continual presence in mine. Having made my wishes perfectly clear for all those years, I was confident the Father had and would continue to grant that which I prayed devoutly for, even if the prayer was out of my own fear and selfishness in not losing what mattered most to me. But little did I neither know nor want to know then that the fifty year celebration in their beloved Church of Mount Carmel would be their final good-bye while alive.

After more than three-quarters of a century residing in Mount Vernon, my parents were ready to move. Or were they? Their brief stay at the senior apartment building on Third Avenue was the impetus to get out of town and get out quick. But would that be the best of reasons?

There were mixed emotions on the day of the move to Flemington, New Jersey. Mom could not wait to get out of the hell-hole apartment, and she practically ran over the movers to get to the car. Yurtz, on the other hand, stood in the middle of the living/dining room area and sobbed. My friend Michelle had come to help drive one of the cars, and thankfully, to assist me pry my father from the floor on which he stood affixed. Mom rode with Michelle, the two chatting non-stop for the entire trek. Yurtz rode with me, crying for at least the first hour. He was inconsolable; torn as I was with this momentous decision that would forever change all of our lives.

For my parents, the transition from city life to country life was difficult in and of itself, but the aspect of the new location was compounded to the nth degree by all that had been left behind – family, friends, and familiar surroundings. Everyone and everything they had known and loved for over seventy-five years was gone in one car ride and in a mere two hour span of time. Short of ones own death, this was as traumatic an event as could have befallen them.

Mom and Yurtz moved into their new place on Yorkshire Drive in April of 1993. They were lonely in their cul-de-sac seclusion far from the beaten track of city life where every need and every want, especially sisters Nancy and Julie, were a five minute walk away. In such social isolation, their moods swung with the certainty of a pendulum causing situations that were unanticipated and unplanned for.

McDonald's became their daily hangout where they found salvation among those they befriended there. But for the most part, new friendships were difficult to come by in a small town where the inhabitants had been a tight-knit group since childhood, such as the friendships Mom and Yurtz left behind in Mount Vernon. Although they did befriend the company of a few new people, Mom insisted, when questioned as to why she did not get together with them more often, they "are not my friends," the message being that these were not her lifelong, inner circle of cronies from Mount Vernon.

Life in Mount Vernon held to the promises of a big city in that each day would be a buzz with non-stop activity, which, for my parents, brought joy and an eager anticipation of being in the thick of and part of the flurry of action. Mom reveled with pride at having been selected a District Leader for the Democratic Party, a role she devoted herself to with the vigor of a twenty year old. Filled to the maximum with varied activities shared with family and friends, Mount Vernon kept the two senior citizens spry, alert, and happy.

To be torn from amidst the hub so late in life was a turning point from which there would be no return. With their world overturned, they rapidly declined in spirit and in health. Still vibrant and with so much life yet to pursue new adventures, they became more fragile, sedentary, and depressed.

Mom, who had been overly anxious to get to her new address, quickly became disenchanted with it threatening to return to Mount Vernon. Yurtz quietly accepted his fate with resignation, becoming less talkative and the guy without a joke a minute. Mom complained that "he never speaks to me anymore," and all my prodding to "talk to Mom," fell on deaf ears. Yurtz became painfully quiet to the point of mental reclusion, a situation that had been festering since he lost the ability to play his horn and had become more pronounced after the move.

With the lack of physical and mental stimulation, Mom's body gave-way to the dreaded diabetes. Able to control the condition with diet for over thirteen years, it exploded to its full-blown state requiring daily injections of insulin. Her back, which had caused much pain throughout her life, hunched to the point of requiring her to use a walker for stability.

Since childhood I viewed Mom as our family's stabilizing column, her inner strength evident in her every action. No matter the situation, when Mom decided on a particular course, there would be no stopping her from completing her mission. She was determined, head-strong, and forth-right, and there was never a need to question her motive – the well-being of her family.

I shutter to think that Mom may not have been fully aware of how much she was needed, appreciated, and loved. When a friend of mine once observed, "you always kiss and hug your father before your mother," I was hit squarely between the eyes having never realized that as being the case. Yes, the truth is that I tended to be more demonstrative towards my father, a passive, over sensitive soul. He was, after all, my childhood caretaker, and I shared his emotional rollercoaster on a daily basis. Even as a child I felt that Mom had the strength to take good care of herself, but Yurtz needed me in his corner. In light of that, it was no wonder that Mom often said, "you love your father more." When I think of that now, it makes me wonder if Mom ever knew how much she was really loved. Just the thought of that, even now, makes me cry.

From the day of my friend's eye-opening comment, I made certain to alternate who received the first kiss and hug. I loved both parents equally, but it was not until both fell ill and required my aide at bedtime each evening that I treated them equally. I tucked them into bed as they had tucked me in as a child, and I whispered to each as I kissed their cheeks, "I love you."

It was a tumultuous time of profound mental and physical changes for the three of us. In the five years my parents resided in New Jersey, they were under the continued care of fifty-three doctors/surgeons and ingesting, inhaling, and injecting twenty-four medications. There were numerous hospitalizations for surgeries such as the grapefruit-size hernia Yurtz almost expired from and Mom's cataract removals from both eyes. Both needed emergency hospitalizations with several bouts each suffering from pneumonia and congestive heart failures. Yurtz's leg blood clots, macular degeneration, stroke, punctured lungs from a car accident and asthma attacks along with Mom's foot and back sores, numbness in her extremities, and diabetic attacks fed the states of mild depression to exasperated full-blown depressions. I did not recognize their sign, as I, myself, was in a deep depression I was unaware of at the same time. Be it for different reasons, Mom's and my depressions resulted in similar ends – sadness, edginess, weight gains, and a propensity towards outbursts of flared tempers. Yurtz was in a state of continual sadness. Unable to help myself, I was numb as to how to help them.

But thankfully all was not totally gloomy. Before the physical and mental aliments overwhelmed the three of us, there were times of extraordinary joy bonding us ever closer. Together we enjoyed Big Band concerts at Deer Path Park and at Raritan Valley Community College. It was at the college that we heard the marvelous Marine Band in their annual concert honoring Marine Sergeant John Basilone, a World War II hero killed in action. When I contacted the Marine Band Master requesting he consider playing and taping Yurtz's four marches, I was not expecting a reply let alone the one I received.

"The band would be honored to play and record your father's arrangements. Please forward the arrangements in care of myself. The band and I look forward to providing you with the ideal gift for his birthday. Thank you and Semper Fidelis – Master Sergeant J.S. Jacob."

An additional letter and the tape arrived just in time to celebrate Yurtz's seventy-ninth birthday. The present was a perfect one, as Yurtz came alive during the audio as he tapped his foot through the entire recording.

Even the simplest of times together were precious then and more so now when I think back on them. We loved the crisp fall afternoons at Peddlers Village chuckling at the silly but award winning scarecrows that encircled the complex. In winter we braved the cold to marvel at the gingerbread houses enclosed in the Village gazebo. When asked if they wanted to go to a flea market for the first time in their lives, Yurtz said he was not interested in "buying any fleas." And as far as going shopping was concerned, Yurtz nixed the venture. "I'll never send your mother window shopping again." Always his straight-man, I came back with the patented, "Why not?" "Because," he explained, "the last time she went window shopping she bought four windows." Although that joke was "as old as the hills" and we had heard it countless times, we laughed anyway. With that, we continued our stroll through the Lambertville flea market re-living days gone by with the myriad of antiques that made us wonder where the dealers "got that stuff we threw out years ago."

A wonderful day out found us taking a relaxing train ride from Flemington to Lambertville which culminated in an early dinner at the Lambertville Train Station Restaurant, a favorite eatery not only for the food but more so for the beautiful setting of this historic building where we sat by the windows overlooking the quaint town. There were times we rode through the countryside, stopping at Buddy's for a refreshing ice cream. Other times we sat on our deck playing cards then moving our seating positions to take advantage of the shaded areas. Reminiscent of our younger days at 105, Sunday mornings were spent around the television watching old movies, a favorite one being the biographical tear-jerking story of trumpeter Red Nichols and his Five Pennies Band.

No matter what the day held in store, we always managed to continue our five-hundred rummy card game, as cards along with playing the numbers and the horses were part of who we were. Whether it was informally betting on the Kentucky Derby, the Preakness, or The Belmont Stakes or playing friendly games of rummy, black-jack, poker, yahtzee, and any game involving numbers, Mom always had the upper hand, beating Yurtz and me ninety percent of the time. When her hand was itchy, she was definitely a winner. In fact, she was luckiest when I went to college, and she needed the money most.

For my parents, the happiest times in New Jersey were the visits from family and friends from New York. My cousins Theresa, Eric, Erica, Danny, Anna, Toni, and Dennis were here so often they could have used our zip-code as their own. My parents never laughed as loud or as hard as when they stopped by, many times as a surprise and always a welcomed one. And I consider my cousins as sisters and brothers as they provided their shoulders in times of need and their bright lights in times of happiness. I can never fully show my gratitude for all the happiness they brought my parents who sparkled and came to life every time they visited.

When Yurtz was in the sub-acute center for months on end, Theresa gave her Uncle Philly a wake up call every morning whereupon she would sing him a song. The problem, which she fully acknowledges, is that she is tone-deaf. For a person unable to hit one recognizable note in any key to attempt to croon to the man with a perfect ear for tone and quality of tone would have normally been disastrous for the listener. In this case, however, it was a welcomed discord. Well before the finale, both would be belly laughing. Theresa's daily aria was the highlight of Yurtz's day and his best medicine. He loved every last off-key, off-pitch bellow and could not wait for the next day's serenade.

While making a piano tape of Yurtz's love songs, a friend of mine was so inspired by the haunting melodies that she shared the songs with her friend Tessa Bell, a hopeful cabaret singer. As a cancer survivor, Tessa was living her dream of becoming a cabaret performer, and upon hearing Yurtz's music, she soon included two of his love songs in her shows. The most notable show was held in a New York City nightclub and garnered rave reviews. This prompted Tessa not only to include *For You Alone* on her debut CD but to use Yurtz's original song as her title track. The haunting melody captivated audiences wherever Tessa performed, and I had requests from other cabaret singers to allow them to include Yurtz's music in their shows. For Tessa a dream was realized, but for Yurtz, who expressed gratitude to Tessa, it was just too late to revive his youthful dreams. The spark flickered out years before.

37

Signs

It is yet difficult for me to comprehend the finality of death even after the passing of my parents ten years ago. Mom passed on April 30, 1999, and to some extent, Yurtz did likewise on that day. He became a shell of a man, unresponsive to those, including me, attempting to keep him from sinking deeper into the abyss. It was during this time he uttered a phrase that punctured then shattered my heart. The sharp-edged fragments tore at my soul like no other statement before or since. In one of his darkest moments, Yurtz lamented, "I'm sorry I never gave you anything."

Although I questioned the meaning for such a depressing untruth, he expounded no further, and only repeated himself. The words, "I'm sorry I never gave you anything," pounded back and forth in my head echoing countless times on countless sleepless nights. Like a continual migraine, the pain of those words sickened me. I could neither begin to imagine nor begin to comprehend where or how this dreadful notion arose. Unsuccessful in securing explanations, I attempted to decipher the message for myself. Perhaps Yurtz meant he never gave me the materialistic things of life. After all, he never did buy me a two-hundred carat Tiffany emerald pendant encircled with diamonds – nor did he ever present me with a candy apple red convertible, chauffer-driven

Lamborghini. In that context – and only in that context – would there be truth to his statement.

I pondered how my hero, my side-kick for fifty-four years could not have known how he enriched my life with what mattered most – unconditional love and a set of life-defining values that live within me everyday. In that context, he and Mom gave me more than any one child ever deserved, and I could not have wanted for more. They provided me with the opportunity to live a life full of riches far beyond the monetary limits of emeralds, diamonds, cars, and meaningless fancies. The record needed to be set straight lest he leave me not only unfulfilled musically but more importantly unfulfilled in how he enriched my life.

I reminded him everyday of the blessings he and Mom gave me, how much I loved them, and how they would live on in me. Knowing Gene and I had spent hours at the hospital, our dear friend Wendy arrived with a large pizza in hand. The aroma of Yurtz's beloved garlic, tomato gravy filled the air, and he took his last breaths passing in my arms with a smile on his face and a wink of his eye. Just six months after Mom left me, my world totally collapsed as the music died on October 22, 1999.

The nurse attempted to calm the woman now crying like the baby girl she once had been and who was now holding on for dear life. "He's happy now," she said as she stroked my head and held my hand. And true to my selfishness as an only child, I retorted, "But I'm not!"

Summoned, the doctor arrived within minutes. The form of an unfamiliar man stood before us, as he was not one of the fifty-three doctors we had come to know over the past few years. He bowed his head acknowledging our grief, "I am sorry for your loss." Still holding my daddy and crying like a baby, I nodded in response. It was then that the doctor introduced himself. "My name is Dr. Schwartz."

Without pausing, he continued describing what his function was, but not one of the three of us heard anything after his name. In case I had not processed what was said, Gene pointed it out again. "This is Dr. Schwartz!" A hospital filled with many hundreds of doctors, and "Dr. Schwartz" arrived to lift me from the depths. It was a moment of levity as the three of us started laughing at the thought of Yurtz telling his most famous and my favorite joke. "I called the office of Schwartz, Schwartz, Schwartz, Schwartz, and Schwartz!"

Maybe the nurse had been correct. Yurtz was happy now, and although trying to comfort his daughter from his new bandstand, the moment of levity was short-lived. I sobbed.

When my parents passed within six months of each other, I was incapacitated. Becoming an orphan is devastating at any age, but for this only child such a profound loss was the nightmare I dreaded since childhood. My array of emotions boiled to the brink even spilling over to the anger I felt directed at the Father for not having fulfilled my Novena prayers. What constitutes a long and healthy life? And how in reality can my parents stay with me forever? My unrealistic expectations superseded common sense in my plea for a forever with me status. But, at the risk of being perceived at incapable of rationality, I choose to believe that He is still granting my wishes in the metaphysical form of signs sent to me, perhaps Dr. Schwartz the first of many. My daily diary details astounding events that coincidence alone can not explain and which prove, if only in my mind, that my parents are with me to this day. In my darkest hours of need and in unexpected times as well, the signs are revealed, their calming effect equated to sedative meditations and are unparalleled in their influence upon me. Perhaps one day those writings will produce a second text, but, for now, I have selected to reveal that which I consider the most surreal of incidences.

In the quest to locate long, lost family in the homeland of my ancestors, the circumstances of that quest is the test of faith in the supernatural. What began on paper as a routine two week vacation blossomed into a month-long adventure of epic proportions. Although novices in European travel, Gene and I ventured forth luggage in hand, packs on our backs, limited Italian verbiage, and mass transit as our only means of transportation. After delightful visits to Milan, Lake Como, Venice, Florence, Siena, Assisi, and Rome, we headed East of Naples towards the Campobasso region of Italy with the hope of family contact. To this point throughout all of Italy, English had been spoken by most of the locals, but it became quickly evident that all of the passengers and the crew on board the train to Campobasso spoke only in native tongue, a tell-tale indication of the remoteness of the area we had entered.

From the train station in Campobasso, we hailed the only non-rail transport we had to take in order to trek the rest of the way to the mountain town of Castropignano, a twenty minute drive from civilization as we know it. Zigzagging up the steep terrain, we finally reached the cloud base where the Hotel Palma stood majestically perched overlooking the valley below. The massive two hundred room hotel complex included four dining rooms each easily able to service three to five hundred people, and outdoor pool, tennis courts, and a game room large enough to contain three normal size basements. It was perfect. Or was it?

The parking lot was empty, as were the courts, the pool, and the entire area surrounding the building. Except for the two of us and the driver, the area was eerily void of people. The driver removed our belongings from the car, wished us well, and drove off down the mountain leaving us no choice but to venture into the building lest we spend the night stranded outside in no-man's land.

Feeling a tad apprehensive, we entered into another world. The lobby was dark, and the check-in desk unattended. We searched for any form of life. "Is anyone here?" Gene's voice echoed off the walls. "Is anyone here?"

With no response, we peered through two doors leading into a dimly lit dining hall, and in the far reaches of the hall, we noticed the figure of a man in a smaller, adjacent room. "Hello. Is anyone here?" Gene summoned again attempting to catch the attention of the man in the corner room.

Spotting us in the doorway, the man acknowledged us. "Ciao!" he yelled as he ran towards us waving his hands frantically. "Ciao!"

As he approached, our misgivings were somewhat relieved as we could see his smiling face beaming with elation at our presence. Slight of build and donning a chef's apron, the gentleman began orating a mile-a-minute, and had he been communicating in English rather than Italian, we may have comprehended considerably more than just his name – Mario. We stood there nodding our heads yes as if we did understand – just as my cousins use to do when Grandma Toot-Toot talked to them. Practically raised in Grandma Toot-Toot's house as a child, I understood Italian quite well then but not quite so well forty years removed from it. Nonetheless, Mario's grandiose hand gestures along with the Italian that was decipherable, I figured that he wanted us to go to our room, freshen up, and return to the grand ballroom for lunch.

As we made our way to our second floor room, it became quite apparent that we were the only two hotel guests. *What have I gotten us into?* I thought as we unpacked the few items we had. Opening the floor to ceiling shutters, the lack of oxygen above the cloud line and a panoramic view of the mountain-valley vista took our collective breath away.

Mario met us in the lobby and escorted us to a table for two in the far reaches of the dining hall where he presented us with a four-course feast for the taste buds. Scurrying back to our table, the red liquid of the Gods in hand, Mario began stomping his feet and proudly pointing to himself. We chuckled at Mario's comical rendition of the dance of the grapes reminding us of the famous Lucille Ball grape mashing scene. But even as the third bottle of homemade Montepulciano arrived at our table, the level of anxiety I was feeling could not be diminished even if Mario had indulged us with a vat of his brew. We were alone and without command of the language or access to a vehicle to navigate two towns north to the more remote mountaintop village of Casalciprano where we were not even certain family still existed. We became increasingly quieter, each mentally wondering what we were doing there.

I finally broke the ice. "I'm sorry, Gene, for getting us into this situation."

"Let's think of these three days as a rest stop. We've been on the go for two and a half weeks non-stop. We're here now, so we'll make the best of it. Let's think of this as another part of our adventure. We'll be nice and rested before we go to Sorrento."

Even Gene's positive spin on the circumstances could not perk me up. "Thanks, but I'm still upset and angry at myself for dragging both of us so far off the beaten track. I tried so hard to plan the trip, and every part of the trip has been perfect up until now. We're on a wild goose chase because I wanted to find family that I'm not even sure still live here. I'm sorry," I apologized again.

"We'll be okay," Gene assured as he took another sip of wine. I lowered my head so he would not see the tears forming.

Mario raced towards the lobby, and talking excitedly to people other than the two of us, we heard him announce, "Gli Americani sono qui! Gli Americani sono qui!"

The dining hall doors swung open so forcefully they nearly slammed into the wall. The people Mario had been engaged with came bounding into the hall, the man lagging far behind the woman who was headed directly towards us. Before we could place our wine glasses on the table, the woman pounded her coffee mug on top of our table nearly spilling its contents. "Do you mind if I join you for awhile?" she rhetorically inquired as she pulled a chair up to the table and sat down before we could respond.

"Not at all. Please join us," we quickly offered with immediate sighs of relief in response to someone speaking perfect English.

"My name is Francesca." Waving her companion over, she continued. "And this is my husband, Franco."

Franco reached out to shake hands as Gene introduced us to the new couple sharing our table. Before we could get another word in edgewise, Francesca, in the space of two minutes, spouted out a brief summary of their life history.

"I was born and raised right here in this town. I've known Mario my whole life. He's a dear friend – actually more like family. Franco grew up in Rome. After we married, we lived in Italy for awhile before moving to what is now our permanent home – Ottawa, Canada. Every so many years we come back to Italy to visit our families and friends here. Today, we were on our way to a different town, but since we just happened to be in this area and were so close, we decided to pay Mario a surprise visit. So, what are you two doing here?"

After a brief summary of our deplorable situation, Francesca chimed in, "Casalciprano? That little village is two towns away. You can't get there without a car. And believe it or not, I've lived in this area and have never been there. We'd love to take you there, wouldn't we, Franco?"

Before we could play a round of Bocce, we were in their Mercedes and on the narrow, winding road to Casalciprano. Upon arrival, we became a bit of a curiosity as the heads of the locals started to pop out of windows and doors to get a glimpse of the strangers in their tiny village.

With friendly, enthusiastic aggression, Francesca knocked on doors and stopped the locals in their tracks in an attempt to get a lead as to the whereabouts of the priest Father Don Elreo Petti, Yurtz's first cousin. After numerous disappointing inquiries, Francesca discovered that Father Elreo's church was in an even more remote town – if it was possible to be even more remote – and would not be returning anytime soon. Persistent in her detective work, Francesca finally received information useful to our search.

We climbed the steep incline to the house where two Petti families supposedly resided. When repeated knocks at the door failed to produce a response from within, it was time to retreat. We had all but given up hope of contacting family when we spotted a young woman coming up the street towards us. Smiling and emitting hospitable vibrations, she was a welcomed sight. With the word getting around quickly in a small town, she had heard of our inquiries. Introducing herself, Maria Petti informed us that she and her mother-in-law, Wanda Petti, lived in the two story dwelling. My heart pumped wildly as Maria opened the door inviting us in. Standing at the top of the staircase stood the noble Wanda, a beautiful, elderly lady dressed head to toe in black, reminding me of Grandma Toot-Toot who dressed likewise for the full sixteen years of mourning she endured after Grandpa Toot-Toot passed.

We later discovered that Wanda purposely did not answer the door because she sadly thought the Americans had come to rob her. Little did she expect that all I had hoped to steal was a hug.

Maria prompted us to go upstairs; Wanda led us to the dining room. Fluent in Italian and in English, Francesca became the interpreter, explaining to each side what the other side was saying. Gene and Franco sat quietly at the table observing the proceedings. As familiar as a few of the names seemed, it had been so long ago when the family parted, my grandparents opting for a life in America, that Wanda was not making connections.

Gene reminded me of the family photo album I had compiled and brought along on the trip. The first photo was of Yurtz's parents – Grandpa and Grandma (Petti) Lucchini. Wanda recognized the names but not the photos of the young, newly wed Petti-Lucchini couple. Turning to the next page in the album, I revealed in English as

Francesca flawlessly restated in Italian, "This is my Great Grandfather, Nunzio Petti."

Suddenly pushing back in her chair and grasping at her heart, Wanda gasped for air. She lit up as though on fire, and I feared I had inadvertently caused the little woman a heart attack on the spot. Wanda jumped up from her seat, turned sharply, and pointed to a large photograph on the dining room wall behind her seat. "Nunzio Petti," she gasped again still holding her heart. With tears gushing forth and her fire still ablaze, she pointed at the photo in my album and to the one on the wall. "Nunzio Petti! Nunzio Petti!"

There it was plain as the sun in the sky - the original picture of Nunzio Petti. We had been so intent on name recollection then on my album that neither Gene nor I noticed the picture on the wall. The connection was made; a moment that still sends chills up my spine. There we were together for the first time – Nunzio's granddaughter and great-granddaughter. We fell into each other's arms and sobbed.

Francesca and Maria joined us in a good cry. Gene thanked Franco for the incredible moment of a lifetime and the miracle reunion which, without Francesca and Franco, would never have taken place.

Maria immediately served coffee and pastries, and through Francesca, our interpreter, we spent the next two hours talking and looking over the photo album of the Petti-Lucchini clan from America. Francesca and Franco were thoroughly engrossed and elated at the outcome of our meeting, but due to their previous plans, it was finally time to leave. Realizing we would not be able to get back to Casalciprano, Gene and I presented Wanda with gifts to share with the rest of the family – the photo album, three CD's of Yurtz's original music, and three sets of Christmas ornaments from America. Amid the tears, we left.

On the way back to the hotel in Castropignano, Franco took a short detour to a vineyard and fig tree area. We picked and ate figs right off the trees, and it so reminded me of Grandpa Toot-Toot and Uncle Dominick who had gargantuan, prize-winning, scrumptious figs growing in the backyard on Bond Street. That evening, upon the recommendation of Francesca and Franco, we dined in the only pizza/ restaurant in town where homemade, fresh daily specialties were so divine we ordered, via sign language, meat lasagna for the next evening as well.

The following morning was drab and drizzly, but although the weather was uncooperative, our spirits from the day before could not have been any sunnier. We strolled into town stopping at the post office and the only two local stores therein. We made our way to the remains of an old castle and then to the cemetery where photographs of the deceased and eternal lights graced every monument. Both places were most fascinating, and the views from the top of the town magnificent. We returned to the still empty hotel, and as we contemplated how to spend the next nineteen hours, the phone rang. A sweet voice was on the line attempting with much difficulty to speak English in the midst of Italian. With intense concentration I gathered the essentials. "My name is Wanda. My dad is Giuliano. Giuliano is the son of the Wanda you met yesterday. Can we come visit you at the hotel now?"

At that moment, the sun was at its fullest intensity for me. Gene and I quickly freshened up and waited their arrival in the lobby. I was pacing the floor when three people appeared at the door – Wanda's son Giuliano and his two daughters Wanda and Erica. Introductions were accompanied by hugs, as is the traditional Italian greeting whether in Italy or America. With the photo album in Giuliano's hand and a one-ton weight Italian-English dictionary in Wanda's grip, we communicated as best we could. Before any of us realized it, nearly three hours had vanished.

Since we had left gifts the day before, Giuliano returned the favor with a gift for us – a poster of their family band, Mille Luci. When I spotted Giuliano kneeling in the front of the band holding a trumpet, I lost control of my emotions. How unbelievable that my dad and me and our cousin 7,000 miles away play trumpets. The music tradition of our family lives.

Before my new three cousins left the hotel, they invited me and Gino, Gene's new Italian nickname, to lunch the next day to meet the rest of the family. Giuliano and his daughter Wanda, still anchored to her dictionary, picked us up mid-morning. We drove to Giuliano's house where his wife Dora, son Manuel, the elder Wanda, Maria, and even Father Don Elreo were waiting with open arms. After snacks, which in American would have been considered a full breakfast, Giuliano took us on a grand tour of the magnificent town of Casalciprano. It was truly the most beautiful town we had been to in Italy, not because it was the home of my ancestors, but because it truly was. In addition to the stunning views of the mountainous countryside, there were fresh flowers on all the windows of each house, bronze monuments commemorating town festivals, etchings depicting scenes on the polished granite town walls, beautiful tiles of significant events of the town, and several glass enclosed rooms housing scenes of life as it had been hundreds of years ago.

Our cousins proudly showed us Great Grandfather Nunzio Petti's tavern, the first tavern-store built in the town, as well as his original home – both buildings still as they were in the early eighteen hundreds. But the crown jewel of the tour ended in the church housing one thousand year old carved wooden statues. Father Don Elreo gave us the grand tour of the church where Grandma Marianne Petti and Grandpa Felice Lucchini were married. We were in awe and totally mesmerized by the whole experience. What an incredible feeling to be standing in all of those sacred places.

Lunch was served with the entire family gathered around the lengthy table, and with the aid of Wanda's dictionary, hands waiving, eye contact, and huge smiles, we managed to have conversation with at least some understanding of the conversation. Even elder Wanda was telling then laughing at her own stories causing the rest of us to laugh with her. There were times all of us were laughing so hard, our collective ribs hurt.

After seven hours of pure joy with the most beautiful, giving, loving family that we had been blessed to come to know, it was time to leave. Amid the hugs, kisses, tears, hugs, kisses, and more tears, we finally waved good-bye with the promise to return. As I looked back from the car window, I saw elder Wanda's figure waning as the distance between us widened. She continued throwing kisses and wiping her eyes, and I reciprocated likewise until she faded out of view. It was a rather quiet ride back to the hotel. Still trying to process the events of the past three days, I was not really ready to leave my wonderful cousins. I cried the rest of the way.

That evening at dinner, Gene and I relived the experiences of those three days, the discussion honing in around the possibility of a higher intervention favoring our pursuit of family. Could the events leading us to family in the remotest area of the Italian countryside have been purely coincidental or could there have been a power beyond that which we can truly comprehend? With a diary filled with unusual, unexplained phenomena regarding my parents contacts with me after their passing, I believe that their spirit, their energy, their force, or whatever else it could be called, is with me, and that I have not been forsaken by the Father who has granted my Novena prayers in ways beyond the scope of physicality to a metaphysical level.

Gene, a non-believer in those matters, could generally rationalize events, but his usual skepticism in and denial of the area of the supernatural had him pondering and questioning this episode. Alone in a massive two-hundred room hotel with no transportation and little grasp of the native tongue, we had reached a painful dead end in a quest to meet those who we had never known. To abort our mission seemed to be our only option at the time, lest a miracle occur. How else could we explain the mysterious appearance of Francesca and Franco all the way from their home in Ottawa, Canada – at that remote Italian outpost – at that very moment in time – on that very day? Gene and I agreed that Mary and Phil, our Guardian Angels, had sent them to show us the way. You may choose to conclude otherwise. We choose to believe in miracles.

38

The Affirmation

The events in Italy that led us to family are true. Francesca and Franco were real. The energy force that connected them to me was the miracle of my Guardian Angels, my parents.

A year after our trip to Italy, the confirmation of my belief was realized. In search of important documents requested for the issuance of visas for an up-coming trip to Russia, I stumbled across my parents' 1917 and 1919 birth certificates. With the names of their **Godparents (Sponsors)** clearly scribed on the nearly one-hundred-year old documents, I had my confirmation.

Certificate of Baptism

✝

CHURCH OF

Our Lady of Mount Carmel

MOUNT VERNON, NEW YORK

—•◄◙• This is to Certify •◙►•—

That ___ Mary Curto

Child of ___ Angelo

and ___ Santa Groccia

born in ___

on the ___ 25th ___ day of ___ December ___, 1919

was

Baptized

on the ___ 22nd ___ day of ___ February ___ 19 20

According to the Rite of The Roman Catholic Church

by the Rev. ___ Cherubino Viola, O.F.M.

the Sponsors being { Domenico Befano
{ Francesca Groccia

as appears from the Baptismal Register of this Church.

dated ___ October 9, 1980

Rev. Simon Drulfani Pastor

Comm: ___

Conf: ___

Marriage ___ to Felice Lucchini on Feb. 7, 1943

212

Certificate of Baptism

✝

CHURCH OF

Our Lady of Mount Carmel

MOUNT VERNON, NEW YORK

⸺⊷ This is to Certify ⊶⸺

That   Felice Lucchini

Child of   Felice

and   Anna Maria Petti

born in

on the   8th   day of   February   1 917

was

Baptized

on the   8th   day of   March   17   19

According to the Rite of The Roman Catholic Church

by the Rev.   Alberto Matteucci

the Sponsors being {   Domenico Piazza
               {   Raffaela Di Francesco

as appears from the Baptismal Register of this Church.

dated October 9, 1980

(signature) Pastor

Comm:

Conf:

Marriage to Maria Curto on February 7, 1943

.

Epilogue 1

In November of 2008, our adopted Native American Navajo daughter, Alberta, gave birth to a beautiful baby boy. With that wonderful news, Ali also delivered the surprise and honor of a lifetime. Our new grandson was given the name Skyler Lucien **Lucchine** Cohoe. My mother, I am certain, is beaming with delight on her new great grandson. She finally has the Lucchine heir she had promised Pop.

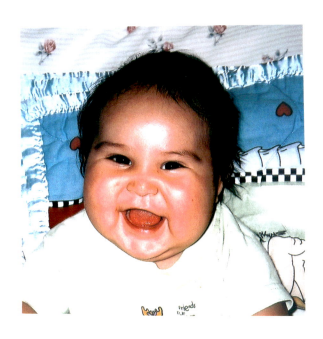

Epilogue 2

Since the passing of my parents ten years ago, I have found solace in my continued correspondence with their dearest friends, whose words not only comfort me in my darkest hours but whose words lift me with an incomparable joy knowing how the lives of so many were profoundly touched by the presence of my parents on Earth.

The words of Judy Marini were echoed by many of Mom's friends.

"Mary had the gift of brightening up the room with her presence. I admired her sense of loyalty to family and friends. She was a special lady, and I feel privileged to have had her in my life."

The woman I admired most was best eulogized by friend Pearl Stockbarger.

"Mary created forever memories, and the sweetness of them will be a lasting legacy of her goodness and graciousness. God, I know is nodding – Mary you have done well."

Yes, Mom, you have done well, and if there is a special section in heaven for those who have been inspirational and who have brought joy to others, you, my beloved mother Mary, are in that section as the ultimate role-model for all that is good about human-kind.

And in communiqués with my dad's numerous friends similar messages offered me comfort as well.

The sentiments of Emil Paolucci, former President of Musicians Local #38, were reiterated many times over.

"If there is a Hall Of Fame for Comedians and Musicians in Heaven, Phil is already in both and on their executive boards."

Quentin Solano, Executive Board Member of Musicians Local #38, added the following:

"The Maestro is with the Big Band up there and no doubt the leader of the group."

In my heart I know the truth of those statements and therefore will continue to put in my request:

Play Me A Song, Daddy!

Play Mom And Me A Song.

Printed in the United States
219241BV00001B/5/P